IN PRAISE OF THE USELESS LIFE

"This beautiful book is both simple and profound, written with humor, a grounded sense of humanness, and luminous attention to what lies at the heart of things. After turning the last page, you might, as I did, sit for a while caught by the mystery and meaning of your own life."

Sue Monk Kidd

"Paul Quenon may describe the monastic life as 'useless,' a life of play, and that is often how its critics describe it. But he's written a book that strikes me as valuable in a culture so terribly marred by narcissism. The key to monastic life, as his novice master Thomas Merton advised him, is 'to live the life here at the monastery, stop looking at myself, and forget myself.' In an anxious age, we need to be reassured that 'the best thing is to take in one breath at a time. . . . Every breath comes from God, and the air supply is unlimited.' As we wrestle with faith in a world that ignores or denounces it, we need to be reminded that 'prayer is a breathing that purifies the air, like leaves on the tree.' Monks, as people of prayer, may be useless, but this book is evidence that they are also necessary and even indispensable."

Kathleen Norris
Author of *The Cloister Walk*

"Paul Quenon does not romanticize the monastic life. He presents frankly its challenges and pitfalls, and we understand that life can be an unending prayer in the best and fullest sense, even with inevitable, instructive, and mundane annoyances amid the beauty. We may transform our own lives by studying Quenon's."

Fenton Johnson
Author of *The Man Who Loved Birds*

"When, after a year as a novice, Paul Quenon told his novice master that he wanted to become a monk, Thomas Merton replied 'Good.' Good indeed, not only for the poet-monk himself but for all who encounter this generous account of the playful dance of his vocation. Like the lovers in the Song of Songs, Br. Paul calls us to join him outside and learn to live on intimate terms with heaven and earth."

Stephanie Paulsell
Susan Shallcross Swartz Professor of the
Practice of Christian Studies
Harvard Divinity School

"It is sometimes said that monks are ordinary people living an extraordinary life. By granting us a glimpse into the daily, common life of a Cistercian, and describing his own inner journey, Br. Paul Quenon proves that the opposite is also true: monks can be extraordinary people living what comes to be a very ordinary, even 'useless' life by the world's standards."

Cyprian Consiglio, O.S.B. Cam.
Author of *Prayer in the Cave of the Heart*

"I have learned more sitting on the porch of Thomas Merton's hermitage with Paul Quenon than I have from many books. This delightful memoir provides a window into a monk and poet's life at Gethsemani recounted with charming anecdotes and fascinating details. Br. Paul has become a mentor for many with his own spiritual message that is grounded in the simple and divine joys of just being alive."

Jonathan Montaldo
Author of *A Year with Thomas Merton*

IN PRAISE OF THE USELESS LIFE

A MONK'S MEMOIR

PAUL QUENON, O.C.S.O.
FOREWORD BY PICO IYER

AVE MARIA PRESS AVE Notre Dame, Indiana

Scripture texts in this work are taken from *New Revised Standard Version Bible*, copyright © 1989 the Division of Christian Education of the National Council of the Churches of Christ in the United States of America. Used by permission. All rights reserved.

"Restless Silence," "Teresa and John," and "The Cowl" excerpted from *Unquiet Vigil: New and Selected Poems* by Paul Quenon, O.C.S.O. Copyright © 2014 by The Abbey of Gethsemani. Used by permission of Paraclete Press. www.paracletepress.com

Dickinson poetry excerpted from *THE POEMS OF EMILY DICKINSON: READING EDITION*, edited by Ralph W. Franklin, Cambridge, Mass.: The Belknap Press of Harvard University Press, Copyright © 1998, 1999 by the President and Fellows of Harvard College. Copyright © 1951, 1955 by the President and Fellows of Harvard College. Copyright © renewed 1979, 1983 by the President and Fellows of Harvard College. Copyright © 1914, 1918, 1919, 1924, 1929, 1930, 1932, 1935, 1937, 1942 by Martha Dickinson Bianchi. Copyright © 1952, 1957, 1958, 1963, 1965 by Mary L. Hampson.

Foreword © 2017 by Pico Iyer

Founded in 1865, Ave Maria Press is a ministry of the United States Province of Holy Cross.

www.avemariapress.com

Paperback: ISBN-13 978-1-59471-759-8

E-book: ISBN-13 978-1-59471-760-4

Cover image © Michael Freeman / Alamy Stock Photo

Cover and text design by Samantha Watson

Printed and bound in the United States of America

Library of Congress Cataloging-in-Publication Data is available.

God alone is worthy of supreme seriousness. But man is made God's plaything and this is the best part of him. Therefore every man and woman should live life accordingly, and play the noblest games and be of another mind than what they are at present. . . . For they deem war a serious thing, though in war there is neither play nor culture worthy the name, which are the things *we* deem most serious. Hence all must live at peace as well as they possibly can. What, then, is the right way of living? Life must be lived as play . . . sacrificing, and singing and dancing.

Plato, *Laws*

What is serious to men is often very trivial in the sight of God. What in God might appear to us as "play" is perhaps what He Himself takes most seriously. At any rate the Lord plays and diverts Himself in the garden of His creation. . . . No despair of ours can alter the reality of things, or stain the joy of the cosmic dance which is always there. Indeed, we are in the midst of it, and it is in the midst of us, for it beats in our very blood, whether we want it to or not.

Thomas Merton, *New Seeds of Contemplation*

You are mad. Yes. The way God is mad. God made the world for the joy of it, not the need of it. It is full of his glory. Still. Despite what we have made of it.

Matthew Kelty, *My Song Is of Mercy*

CONTENTS

Foreword

I knew, before I turned to the first page, that Br. Paul Quenon's reflections on a life of friendship and prayer—of hard
work and song—would be radiant. But still I was taken
aback at how often I had to stop reading *In Praise of the Useless Life* and put the book down to start scribbling notes. Here
is the practical essence of six decades of living in the Cistercian monastery of Gethsemani, amidst the quiet hills of Kentucky, in love with the presents, the Presence, that are hidden
in every moment. Before reading Br. Paul's celebrations, I'd
thought that contemplation was mostly about sitting still
and closing your eyes; after completing his book, I realized
that in truth it's about opening your eyes and awakening to
the beauty all around you. Coming to your senses, in fact,
and finding the grace in red hawks and juniper bushes and
quirky humans that every life can be illuminated by.

I knew Br. Paul's book would be nourishing—and deeply
liberating—because I've been reading his poems and looking
at his photographs for years. But also because I'd been lucky
enough to be taken by a writer friend to Gethsemani, and led
out across the fields to Thomas Merton's old hermitage by Br.
Paul, who'd been a novice under the searching monk-poet
known to his brothers as Fr. Louis. Soon after we got to the
open white house with its roomy porch, Br. Paul shed light
on where we were with some verses he knew by heart, Rilke
and Emily Dickinson. Then he pulled down, at random, a
volume of Merton's journals, lined up on the shelves in the
hermitage, and began to read. Suddenly his novice master's

spirit—frank, questioning, quick with life and wit—was all around us.

The second time I visited, I was fortunate to attend one of the services in Gethsemani's great, light-filled chapel. In between his many duties around the cloister, Br. Paul organized a long evening of poetry and laughter for a group of us in the hermitage, alive with the spirit of fellowship and literary communion that Merton made famous around the world. It was only after I left that I realized Br. Paul had somehow fed us all, with memorably tasty pizza, even as he attended every Office in the chapel—and partook of the sense of play and friendship that dances through this book.

Even after two visits, though, I was touched and instructed by much that Br. Paul shares in these pages. For one thing, he opens the door to everyday life in a monastery and brings the monks we swathe in mystery joyfully down to earth. One of his brothers becomes a chemist for the monks' cheese lab, we read, and lives in his own whimsical hermitage, a used trailer; another is a former clown from a family circus. One oblate is a former Hollywood screenwriter who took the celebrated photograph of the dropping of the atom bomb from within the *Enola Gay*; one novice who leaves eventually becomes a cabinet minister in the Sandinista government. The monk we get to know best is busy organizing exhibitions, teaching in Nigeria, studying photography in Santa Fe, and writing haiku every day. He's climbing power poles and working in the electronics department of the monastery with a former jazz pianist, driving across the country, saying the Divine Office behind the wheel (so long as he's on a straight and empty road).

The monastic life isn't all silence and prayer, we see, nor is it all sweetness and light. Merton and Br. Paul at one point exchange "snide" expressions; yet Fr. Louis also invites the monks to call him "Uncle Louie." And by showing us the power of repetition and habit, Br. Paul expands our notion of time, so that something wider than the moment can enter the everyday recitations and patterns of every one of us.

Our monastic guide, in fact, proves to be as without illusions and as full of down-home humor as his self-deprecating title would suggest. Meditation can lead at times to a "gray funk," he admits, rather than to "quiet lucidity." Silence can be a much-needed respite from "pressure at Mass" and "bother in the kitchen." The monks' lives are as tough and far from otherworldliness as any other hard labor, and Br. Paul is quick to assert that "not much appears there in terms of spiritual excitement, let alone progress."

He's bringing a life of devotion close to us, in short, and in the process reminding us that even those of us out in the world can practice some of the attention and self-surrender that gives the monastic day its depth. We, too, could see humor in the mockingbird serving up a song as we try to sleep; we could choose to spend time being quiet every day; we could commit poems to memory so that something wiser and larger than us speaks through us; we could see that "moths are underrated."

In an age of distraction and forgetfulness and speed, it's no surprise, perhaps, that more and more of us in the wider world are going on retreat, or trying to bring even a little of a monk's discipline and clarity into our overcrowded days. Every time I visit the Benedictine hermitage where I've been staying regularly for twenty-six years, I not only see my life—and love my life—as I never do when caught up in a traffic jam or a rush of emails; I also am reminded that the real-estate agent in the next cell, the social worker next to me in the line for soup, the Buddhist I pass on the monastery road, all have something essential in common. We're joined at the root, even if our paths fly off in a hundred directions.

This is part of what comes home to me as I accompany Br. Paul on his walks, in life and on the page, traveling back to his family kitchen and the long drives he took in his dad's black Chevy as a boy in West Virginia, or when I read him telling us that Merton advised, "Answers are beside the point." It's what I feel when he writes, with such gratitude and delight, of the music of Bruckner or the shades of solitude given soulful voice by Emily Dickinson. The "narrowing of living space," as he writes so beautifully of Dickinson, "seemed to extend the circumference of her mind and heart."

Br. Paul always keeps his window open as he reads, he tells us, and he loves to sleep under the stars. The heavens are everywhere, in short, if only we have eyes to see them. Fresh air is available at every moment. And if monks are just regular folks, so, too, we regular folks can be as steadied as they are by devotion and ritual. Depth is not confined to the enclosure. "Several of the esteemed doctors and masters of my spiritual formation have been trees," Br. Paul writes in a wonderful sentence that, like many here, suggests his fellow connoisseur of stillness and the art of looking, Henry David Thoreau.

We tiptoe, in silence, as we read this book, into a foreign world of "*jubilos*" and "ferial days," into ancient rites and the mystery of psalms sung in the dark. One of the most haunting passages concerns the sense that so many of his brothers had that when Thomas Merton left Gethsemani to travel to Asia, he would never come back. Yet at the same time, Br. Paul is unaffected and grounded enough to remind us that monks can sport Elvis-worthy sideburns—to the horror of other monks—and coin witty one-liners about the joy of procrastination.

In the end, I feel, *In Praise of the Useless Life* opens a door within every one of us. Br. Paul's "vocation" is like being on vacation, he tells us on the first page, alerting us to the fact that the fruits of lifelong contemplation are paradoxical and deep. Secrets hide out inside words and sounds. But by presenting his life in so humble and human a way, he also reminds us that there may be a monk's candle inside every one of us, one that we can keep alive even in the midst of our hectic, stressful, imperfect days in the world. The monk's life, I suspect, as I close this lovely and liberating work, is only our possible life, in disguise.

Pico Iyer
May 2017

INTRODUCTION TO
THE CIRCLE DANCE

I am on permanent vacation. This surprising state of affairs is the life that I have been called to, and it has lasted almost six decades. My good fortune is known as a vocation. Monastic life is essentially a vacating, an emptying out, not unlike vacating an apartment and living without furniture, or even without an apartment. Monastics (men and women) vacate the world and go where people of the world do not want to go and remain. To live in solitude, to be specific, is one of the most difficult things for a person to endure. "Man's unhappiness," as Pascal said, "spring from one thing alone, his incapacity to stay quietly in one room." In more ways than one, that is precisely what I have been doing for a long time—except, rather than inside a room, I prefer to be outside. The generous ceiling of the sky for me is more congenial to solitude, precisely because there I find company with the visible world around me.

But this outward solitude is not enough. Vacating means a personal emptying out of clutter within the mind and heart, certainly a clearing of the nonessential and even some essential furniture to make room for God. A normal home has spouses and maybe children. Life in a monastic community can never be quite the equivalent of a family, although there may be plenty of people around. Radically, there must be an interior journey into a wilderness to be alone, free of the world and at rest in God. Living in cenobitic community might seem to upgrade this desert to the status of a private

1

resort, with all conveniences provided, like laundry and cooking. Perhaps that sounds too good to be true. Well, it is. You will shortly find this is not the case. Everyone here has to put in a hand and do his own part. Work is one of the forms of this emptiness, this vacation. It enhances prayer and keeps it from going static and stale. Likewise, prayer is a form of work—"the work of God," as St. Benedict called it. It requires intention, attention, and persistence.

TEAMWORK

I follow—or stumble along—the "Benedictine way," which approaches life mostly in terms of prayer, work, and reading. To follow all three of these essential principles to the fullest is real work, and indeed at times a hard battle! Key phrases found in the Rule of St. Benedict are "the labor of obedience," "the strong, bright weapons of obedience," "the instruments of good works." It is only when the work of obedience is advanced and matured that we "run the way of God's commandments in the unspeakable sweetness of God's love." I have never been a great runner, but I do like to hike, and have worn out many a pair of boots on the dirt roads and paths up and over what are locally known as "knobs"—too modest to be called hills—on the west side of our monastery land. The knobs are steep enough to pump up breath and heartbeat, but small enough to shortly bring one to good elevation for sight and sense. From my earliest years I climbed, circled back down, saw the monastery steeple appear in the distance above the trees, and knew with increased clarity I wanted to live here, with whatever it offered me at the unseen hand of God.

Work it proved to be, and battle too, but "play" proves to be the fuller truth on this park ground, where St. Benedict says we end up "running with hearts expanded"; dwelling "at rest on the holy mountain"; abiding in the tent where "in his loving kindness the Lord shows us the way of life."

In this regard, the Holy Rule is about a life not far from a maxim in Plato's *Laws*: "Life is to be lived as play." Even more radically speaking, I myself am "God's plaything"— God who "alone is worthy of supreme seriousness." This might sound too Greek, too like pagan fatalism, but to St. Thérèse of Lisieux it was a joy; and so it is to any nun or monk with the heart of a child. It is fun to be a ball tossed about by the hand of Christ. On this Gethsemani Abbey ball field, with its lines and boundaries, there is a constant game going on that gets ramped up by the fact of its having rules and regulations. These rules do make for an intense game, but one's skills over time are dramatically enhanced.

HOLY GAME

In this arena, the biggest game is called liturgy. I can credit my confrere Fr. Matthew Kelty for coaching me broadly into this game analogy and mindset about monastic prayer life and daily activity. Matthew was my senior by age, and my junior in terms of monastic years. He came a year after I entered. We were in the novitiate together. He wrote eloquently of how song, movement, poetry, and music in liturgy are sacred theater. It needs no more substantiation than does a play by Shakespeare or Euripides. In our case, the scripts are coauthored by such ancient masters as that pleading, poignant, and pugnacious bard King David and the immortal narrators Matthew, Mark, Luke, and John, not to mention Isaiah and a stellar rostrum of other prophets and sages.

Why we must carry on this way, day after day, may not be obvious to anyone outside the community. One needs to be inside this chosen life, intensely centered on this space, to understand our odd behavior. It springs from an inner drive as deep as a child's instinct to play, and even more, it rises from a love of life that wants to bring the great inner source of life forward and outward. There is danger herein as well. Like any game, it can be spoiled by a wild, temperamental player or, conversely, by someone rigidly fixated on rules. But when the heat is on, you flow with the rules and just throw yourself into the freedom and play.

I must warn you in advance that I will appear to be playing outside the rules. Even to write this book may seem a broad step outside the enclosure walls and says much that departs from a prescribed script. Well, at least it shows how I've survived, and even thrived, and found a flourishing mode of monastic life. Fr. Matthew has put it quite beautifully:

> We have but to live, take each day as it comes, see the Lord in all that happens and have a kind of response to the will of God that is much like dancing. You must work with it. It is not a matter of passive submission. This no way to dance; it is too heavy, too leaden, too dragging and uninspired. No, you must dance with your partner, you must cooperate, you must work with the will of God. This is the sort of dancing that leads to the kingdom and makes one free.

Thomas Merton, my novice master, had a great capacity for work and play. How else did he write all those books? For him, I suspect, it was a form of play, engaging wit, art, and creativity. Yet much that he wrote demonstrated the strange paradox that out of inner poverty and emptiness come abundant wisdom and great joy.

LIVING FOR THE SAKE OF LIFE

The daily routine of the monastery eventually levels you to the plateau of your ordinariness. There the Word become flesh meets me, precisely where I feel the ache of being human. Although life here can be very busy, once accustomed to the schedule, you have little to divert you from the normal state of affairs, which is a simple quiet and self-forgetting. At least when things are working right, that is the way it is. Ambition and striving fade into the background, and life lived in God is sufficient. To be alive, to move from day to day, to do the chores and greet the smiles of others is a gift and a precious blessing. So gratitude becomes the intrinsic animation of prayer. To live in gratitude simply for being becomes the motif of life, liturgy, and mutual love. It serves no apparent purpose, other than the hidden marvel of being in God. The meaning of love, according to St. Bernard, is love itself. *Amo quia amo.* Why do I love? For the sake of love itself.

For this reason, it is radically a life of play. The purpose of play is play. Despite whatever else you may say about it, play is for exercise, for refreshment, for winning, for community. If play begins to serve an end beyond itself, it ceases to be play. Prayer is much the same thing. Why should I pray? Basically it is for the sake of praying. There is much else we might claim about prayer—it is for the sake of the world, it is for those in need, for the Church, for individual souls—all of which is true. But unless it is rooted in the boundless freedom of love and confidence in God, it is void and crippled. It has some effect perhaps, but lacks the current of grace and graciousness that flows from God.

THE DANCE OF THE LORD

On the day of my solemn vows, Fr. Louis (Thomas Merton) tossed off a quip: "Vows are useless." The funny thing is that one of my two companions at that profession said the same thing to me before the services. I was not thrown off balance by either one of these radical remarks because Fr. Louis had been speaking for months about how the whole monastic life is useless. By then I was ready to lead "the useless life." For all its obligations and demands, its idealism and elaborations, monastic life is a way of entering into the cosmic dance. This primarily requires freedom. As Merton put it:

[L]et go of our own obsession with what we think is the meaning of it all, [that] we might be able to hear His call and follow Him in His mysterious, cosmic dance. . . . For the world and time are the dance of the Lord in emptiness. The silence of the spheres is the music of a wedding feast. The more we persist in misunderstanding the phenomena of life, the more we analyze them out into strange finalities and complex purposes of our own, the more we involve ourselves in sadness, absurdity and despair.

WRESTLING WITH GOD

Another image of monastic life is to say it is a stripping away of the extraneous for the most demanding of sports—wrestling with God. One afternoon I was looking for an explanation of what faith is all about. Fr. Louis told me that faith is a *wrestling*. Jacob wrestled in the darkness with the unseen God. The result of such an intimate engagement was not that Jacob wrested out the secret of God's name. The undisclosed name remained undisclosed. Faith continues to be a struggle in darkness. God gives no answer to the question, "What is your name?" Rather it is our name that is learned, our identity that is changed. In that new identity comes the dawning of a new life. One perhaps that has to be walked with a limp in the hip socket, leaving each of us more vulnerable and weak, but forever marked for having closed in and engaged with totality.

This wrestling is another and tougher kind of game. Christ likewise was a wrestler. Christ in the Garden of Gethsemani was described as being in "agony." The Greek word *agonia* means not "pain" so much as "worked up and sweaty," to the point of dripping blood. In his case it was a tussle of wills—a tussle with the Father whose will would be done.

In a strange leap of the imagination, my most soul-mate poet, Emily Dickinson, elevates this contest to an everlasting competition. Christ and the Father continue in a perpetual go-around after the Ascension:

> He outstripped Time with but a Bout
> He outstripped Stars and Sun,
> And then, unjaded, challenged God
> In presence of the Throne.
>
> And He and He in mighty List
> Unto this present, run,
> The larger glory for the Less,
> A just sufficient Ring.

DANCING WITH GOD

The Holy Trinity, in Greek theology, is described as a perichoresis, a circle dance. As three dancers in one circle, they are dancing as one undivided reality. This dynamic image was translated into Latin with a comparatively static image— the word *circumincession*, indicating a mutual indwelling, a being inside one another. Both images are valid, and both pertain to the Christian life. We engage in the mutual abiding of Christ in the Father and the Father in the Son. Expressed dynamically, we are caught in the flow of the generation of the Son from the Father. In that timeless flow, we are already chosen in Christ, even "before the foundation of the world" (Eph 1:4).

Through this temporal life on earth, with all its twists and turns, the dance and the dancer are becoming one. The pattern I dance and who I am as dancer are indistinguishable. No one knows what the dancer means until the dance is completed. What the dance becomes and how I dance speak of who I am. When action on earth is joined with the larger choreography of heaven, my meaning expands infinitely beyond myself, and I expand along with it. For this to happen, I must get lost in the dance and forget myself. "I have been crucified with Christ; it is no longer I who live, but it is Christ who lives in me" (Gal 2:19–20).

This is partly why a strange exhilaration usually comes over me when somebody I have known well in the community dies. It feels like a cutting free and a circling around. The feeling comes strongly at the end of the funeral. After the final blessing, when the bier is lifted and carried toward the west door to the burial ground, I get excited like a boy getting out of school for summer—a thrill that the training has ended and the real fun has just begun. I certainly felt this strongly at the death of Fr. Matthew Kelty, but it came earlier, a day before the burial. Similarly, when Fr. Louis died, I felt one joyful *Yes!*—in that, at last, he had arrived at the end of the course. The God of perichoresis ever draws us beyond, out into a wide open course—into endless movement, into the limitless depth and height of God. Such ultimately will be "the noblest of games" as Plato says, the circle dance everyone is destined to enjoy.

The following pages are episodes, just a few go-arounds in the life, liturgy, and labor of monastic life. It all happens in the context of the larger, ongoing cycle of the liturgical year, that ritual wheel that turns slowly within the broader cosmic wheel of the earth on its course around the sun. Thanks to the Cistercian order, our monasteries are situated "far from the haunts of men," as expressed in one of our early founding documents. I have lived many years in the country close to the earth, and have acquired a positive sense of traveling a long track around the sun.

When, for example, I awake to the alarm in late February at 2:40 a.m., I see my personal sign again, Scorpio, coming up in the east. Then I recognize I have completed another great round riding this little space car, the Earth. My blood tells me change is coming; the tone of the liturgy moves into challenge, the conflict and dark drama of Lent; then follows a break into the golden blaze of Easter, while grass releases fresh oxygen and trees swell to green. In all, I am carried along by a great dance, and I engage in the dance. And in the end, the dance and the dancer become one.

A Life of Song and Music

Engaging Mind and Body

People sometimes remark on how youthful some older monks look, and I reply that the secret of their vitality is simple: they sing.

Monks stand in choir and sing seven times a day. To breathe often and deeply, to resonate subtly with sound, vibrates all the fibers and is bound to be healthy. It raises the heartbeat and boosts metabolism and soothes the whole system. I generally leave choir feeling energized and refreshed, rather than tired—unless it is one of those excessively long ceremonies. But even on those rare occasions when I feel tired, it's a good tiredness.

Of course, there are other reasons for a monk's youthful appearance: for one, a shaved head is a clever trick for any old man gone gray, and that for us is part of the uniform code. Likewise, a beard masks the folds of a sagging chin. Our vegetarian diet and regular daily schedule keep the animal spirits tamed and relatively contented.

Nature loves habit, which is how habit came to be called second nature. Repeated actions eventually occur instinctively. When the hour comes around for work, prayer, or sleep, a monk's system is ready. Strangely, even prayer feels like a physical need—a spiritual hunger becomes a holy second nature!

To say I need to pray expresses more than a spiritual want; it is a hankering of the body as well. For instance, when I am traveling or otherwise can't get to choir, if time for Terce or None passes me by, I instinctively sense something is missing. My remedy for that was to memorize all the Little Hours psalms so I could recite them alone when I can't get to choir. This has served me well.

KEEPING THE MIND FIT

Memorization as a practice keeps a mind young. It is one vital component of mental well-being. To keep my aging brain from turning into oatmeal, I began to devote a lot of time and effort into recovering Latin and Greek, improving upon something I already knew. I read books by Augustine, Boethius, and Cicero. The mind needs application to work; memory is a kind of mental muscle that can easily atrophy. In our culture, memory goes largely underutilized. Only a couple generations ago, people could recite long poems or songs.

One morning old Br. Claude, while helping the cooks chop vegetables, launched into a whole string of Broadway songs that were so old I had never heard any of them before—tunes that were even pre-World War I. I also recently had the pleasure of listening to a ninety-eight-year-old woman sing "Blue-Eyed Sally" through eight verses—a song I had never heard before.

Most monks in our order memorize a handful of psalms. Every monk knows at least the two regular psalms for Compline (recited every evening in the dark). Frequent repetition of psalms after years of familiarity has its own value. You may ask, does this daily repetition dull the intellect or help it? If constant novelty is the measure of mental agility, then this is a dumb-downer, but if content and quality are the measure, this is a mind builder. Not that we are in choir to develop our minds, but I can testify to the healthy harmony of mind and matter in the very repetition of the psalms for nearly sixty years.

OWNED BY PSALMS

When I entered the monastery in 1958, the liturgy was in Latin. In high school I had two years of Latin, going through Caesar's histories. As a result, in choir I could decipher some of the Latin, but often it amounted to a string of syllables. Nevertheless, the intention of praying, even without understanding, was enough to sustain me. The rounded syllables sounded pleasant enough and left me to pursue my own thoughts and conjectures. The mere act of recitation in a communal effort has its own worth. Not that I advocate a return to Latin, but neither do I dismiss it entirely, especially in regard to Latin set to Gregorian chant. The community here was fortunate to learn from excellent teachers: our own Fr. Chrysogonus Waddell as well as Dom Desroquettes, O.S.B., from Caldey Abbey in England, who was trained at Solesmes Abbey in France.

After Vatican II, we began singing in English. A new frontier opened up. Images and ideas took the foreground of my mind in choir. Eventually, however, as familiarity with the English settled in, recitation became habitual and the old trials of patience returned. Sometimes I follow the meaning, sometimes my mind sinks to a random stream of consciousness, and sometimes I go blank. Verses during psalmody easily pass as an undercurrent casually observed from the lofty bridge of indifference. A phrase in the psalm tosses up, then sinks like a wave. A single word bobs to the surface and disappears, or an entire psalm might slip by ignored. Then something dawns, a sudden epiphany, something clearly speaks to you, or you are speaking in a way truer to the words than usual. Or maybe an insight snaps into view, sparked by a book read that day, something that dovetails with a line in the psalm.

After many years, the psalms have become so familiar that I take them for granted and sometimes fail to hear them. But with persistent attention there comes a new opening where the heart and mind stand behind the words and they become my own. With that grows an inner expansion, a sense that these are not only my words; these are our words. I release and relax into a voice larger than my own, into what has its origin in another. St. Augustine saw in the psalms the voice of Christ. Most of the time I sense this obscurely and implicitly, as a voice not specifically my own, nor specifically of another individual, be it King David, or Asaph, or an anonymous psalmist. I hear the voice of humanity, of any poor loner or derelict, any kind of warrior, someone injured, even vindictive. All of these sentiments, for better or worse, are true of me as well, because they are part of a humanity in which I share. Christ comprehends all this, embraces sinners and saints alike, reaching far beyond my own narrow capacity. Psalmody draws me along, farther and wider, stretches me almost painfully at times, and deepens my empathy for the human race.

How good it is to be stretched beyond your own routine of thoughts and words, to be carried into words you would never say of your own accord—either because they are too lofty or are too crude! Such prayer is no longer personal or private. The boundary of my soul is dissolved; the person I usually am becomes broader; the center of expression is shifted from me to what is beyond, beneath, and around me. Sometimes it feels good to gain circumference, sometimes disagreeable, like being roughly bounced back and forth—like us as kids in the back seat of Dad's black Chevy, long before there were seat belts, driving fast through the West Virginia hills. You couldn't always see what was coming next. Likewise with these ancient psalms: the old Hebrew in the driver's seat doesn't think sequentially or logically, but switches from first person to third and back again. His mood turns on a dime. Balance and beauty are not always the intentions of this primal poetry. Authenticity, grit, and realism are more the order of the day, all spun out in passages of grief and resentment, as well as in sweet trust, love, and serenity—a quiet stroll beside still waters.

This daily practice of psalmody has an additional significance because it carries on something Jesus himself did while on earth. These were the prayers of his family, friends, and fellow Jews, at home, on the road, and in the temple. This prayer continues to belong to his people, and I become identified with them in the present and the past.

Once I wrote a hymn we use for Sext (the 12:15 p.m. Office) during Lent:

> The hour it is when Christ did thirst
> For justice thirsted on a tree.
> His lips were slaked by no relief
> Except a poor man's psalm of grief.
>
> O, by his patience may we share
> The spirit of his saving prayer;
> Through sacred psalms to hunger more
> For justice and its blest reward.

The curious thing is the contrast between the lovely ritual setting of our psalmody in choir and the rough, sometimes bloody content of the psalms—between how we habitually chant in tones smooth, even, and soothing and how we say things abrasive, anguished, torn. The building we stand in is beautiful; monks wear white cowls with long sleeves, in graceful cloaks, bow and rise together, while Vespers light splashes color through western windows onto the wall opposite. Our context creates an effect often contrary to what is actually being said, lamented, complained, bewailed, or cursed. It might overstate it to call it a paradox or a *conjunctio oppositorium*, since usually we hardly revert enough to be aware of it at all. This juxtaposition works indirectly, subtly, on the psyche, imagination, and mind. Some of the effect depends on your own predispositions and on how you assimilate it; you can become pliant or hardened. You can allow yourself to be punched, pulled, and turned like leavened dough by these shifting moods; perhaps you resist, ignore it, or go deaf. I can testify to all these effects. On the whole, however, I leave choir feeling enlarged and more open to life, to the world the way it actually is, to everything held in it for good or ill. What Fr. Louis once said of scripture as a whole can be said especially of the psalms: they show us our humanity.

A Jewish scholar once visited the abbey and asked a small group of us what we meant when we prayed for Zion. For me, the implicit meaning is threefold: the temple in Jerusalem, the Church on earth, and the heavenly Jerusalem. But I seldom remind myself of any of this because all of it is contained in the hope, grief, and joy expressed by whatever psalm I'm singing. Emotions always precede doctrine when scripture is sung.

HOW CAN I KEEP FROM SINGING?

It was my mother who taught me how to sing. I can put myself in that moment. It was in the kitchen by the sink. My twin sister, Eileen, learned immediately after me. We were still just learning how to talk, but it didn't take long to learn to sing, and when Daddy came home that evening we were able to please him by singing. He liked to sing as well, while shaving: "Cool Clear Water" or "Tumbling Tumbleweeds"—the kind of cowboy songs that bespeak the heart of a monk, though he would never know it. My family sang at home when we were washing dishes, or riding on a long trip in the black Chevy.

I was also fortunate to have a home in which classical music could be regularly heard. This is an acquired taste gained early, and we had a few classical records at home, as well as Gilbert & Sullivan, Broadway musicals, and jazz, much of it thanks to my oldest brother, Leonard. Later, when

I started exploring the college library within a ten-minute walk from home, I checked out Beethoven, Tchaikovsky, or organ music by Bach and, with no one else in the house, played them loudly with the lights turned off.

On my first visit to the monastery for an interview, shortly after graduating from high school, I walked into church just while Terce was in progress. The monks were singing the simplest of all Gregorian hymns, the one for the Little Hours on ferial days, one so simple as almost to be nothing but a psalm tone, gentle and direct as any could be. I recognized something in it immediately, how that was the spirit of what I had already been feeling in prayer alone at home. I was amazed that what I was hearing outside me in that music was already inside me previously from silent prayer. It was a perfect correspondence. The interior and exterior were the same. Since then, I have enjoyed that melody countless times, and it is still one I identify with the most readily.

Singing comes naturally to me. Like a bird, I would have to sing even if I didn't have choir. The idea of singing every day in a choir is one of the things that attracted me to the monastery. I liked being in the chorus at St. Peter's High School in Fairmont, West Virginia, where I'm from, and also in the boys' choir. I entered the Trappist order as a choir monk since I knew some Latin and had already acquired a taste for Gregorian chant. Here we engaged in it on a full scale, with all the graduals and responsorials, the lengthy *jubilos* and endless versicles; all was rather demanding but well worth the effort. That full cycle of plainchant was not always so plain, simple, and obvious. It afforded, nevertheless, much of substantial nutrition, immersing me in that ancient, mysterious, inward, and gently modulated world of sound. I am happy we continue to use elements of this in our present liturgy. It needs to be sung to be fully appreciated, for it is designed not for musical effect but to be prayed. It still sets the norm, in my heart, for what monastic liturgy is meant to be.

At Mass, I am content with the role assigned me of singing on the special schola, singing solo, or making intonations. I never had enough "fire in the belly" to persist toward priestly ordination, something of a special vocation within our order. I never entertained dreams of offering Mass, either as a child or as an adult. I never felt captivated, as many priests are, by the thought of offering Mass as their supreme honor in life. For me, to sing and partake with the brothers from the floor feels just right. The fact that I am now dubbed cantor (of sorts) is mostly a result of hanging around here long enough. My musical reading skills and capacity for attention to cues are still wanting.

Many of my reflections and meditations take place while listening to readings at Mass and the Divine Office. Since my mind is not occupied with priestly duties (performing rituals), I am free to quietly compare readings and link ideas and meanings in my mind to get a deeper understanding. It is amazing how new insights frequently jump out at me from stories and lines I have heard hundreds of times. Sometimes current events influence my thinking, like this morning's story of the tower of Babel, where the Lord scrambled the languages of people—this acquired vivid color and relevance from the especially bewildering political atmosphere of today.

EPISODES OF MUSIC

One of those happy chances that occurred after my second year in the monastery was to be given the job of polishing the wooden floor of the church. I did that about once a week with a buffer machine. The organist would practice regardless of my motor noise, and I heard compositions by Bach, Buxtehude, César Franck, and others. I grew to appreciate that job for that reason alone. Later, I became involved in organ tuning and maintenance, thanks to my employment with Br. Kilian Sullivan in the electronics department. I learned how to tune the remote-control pipe organ by tapping each sleeve and refining the length of the pipe so that it was in pitch with the other pipes. We had five organists; of these, one was a jazz pianist from Canada who used to sub-in for Oscar Peterson, and two were graduates of conservatories—Fr. Chrysogonus Waddell in Philadelphia and Br. Francis Kline from Juilliard in New York. On rare occasions the two set aside a morning to hold an organ festival. They practiced for weeks on selected items, either baroque or French romantic, and on the appointed day they lit a candle in front of a Bach icon (one painted at the monastery) and in an empty church, with no audience, performed for an hour. No one was there to listen except the two of them, the angels and saints, and, fortunately, me. I had tuned up the organ.

Theirs was an engagement in pure art! They were playing for the sheer joy of playing, of doing something beautiful in the presence of God, the Blessed Sacrament, and me—a mouse listening in the corner.

Orpheus has occasionally touched me with other such favors, as I was reminded just the other day. Br. Luke Armour was playing a prelude at Mass, and I vaguely recognized the theme. I couldn't place it right away, but then realized it was from the opera *Orfeo ed Euridice*, by Christoph Willibald Gluck. That theme had crossed my mind, coincidentally, the previous day after quite a long absence: "Dance of the Blessed Spirits," which came from the first of the few operas I have attended in my life as a cloistered monk. That was while I was studying in Chicago. The theme was originally written for flute, and the second time I heard it on flute was at a request I made during an extraordinary, enchanted evening deep in the reaches of Mammoth Cave National Park, here in Kentucky—of all places! There I was part of a recording session organized by cellist Michael Fitzpatrick for a CD titled *Compassion*. Ten Tibetan Drepung Loseling monks and I were the singers. Michael played the cello, and the flute was played by Lisha McDuff. The cave was vacated of tourists for our recording, which took place after-hours. We descended a long stairway and walked a quarter of a mile in single-file procession while the Tibetan monks chanted. I had a sense of descending with Jesus into the netherworld after his crucifixion, or of trespassing with Orpheus into the forbidden caverns of Pluto. My part was to sing the triple Alleluias from the Easter Vigil and to recite my poem inspired by Rilke, about Orpheus: "Your music alone, O god of the lyre, soars eternal."

After we finished the recording, I asked the lovely Lisha if she knew the theme from the Gluck opera, and she obliged with a haunting performance right there in the Kentucky underworld, amidst its strange lights and shadows, limestone walls and stalactite ceiling, surrounded by Tibetan monks in maroon and yellow habits, wearing gold, high-crested ceremonial hats. It was hard to believe any of this was really happening. If I had dreamed of such a thing, I would not believe it. I once tried to capture the moment in a poem:

> Here my breathless Alleluias, in triple ascent,
> failed to attain God until
> with bottomless tones you, my Buddhist brothers,
>   rose up
> in measured gradation, to complete some
> obscure code of sound and meaning.

The recording was made and published as a follow-up to the Gethsemani Encounter, a conference organized by the Monastic Interreligious Dialogue in 1996. His Holiness the Dalai Lama attended the meeting, and Michael Fitzpatrick played the cello to begin and end each session. The voice of the Dalai Lama, the chanting of Tibetans, and the English chant of our schola can all be heard.

SOUL BROTHER BRUCKNER

I am in the habit now of regularly listening to great music. I have recently begun going through the symphonies of Anton Bruckner (1824–1896) once more. If there is such a thing as lectio divina (meditative reading), there must also be *audiens divina* (meditative listening). Each evening I listen to one movement, and afterwards turn to regular lectio. Since 1986, I have given ear to Bruckner. Why do I find myself returning to him? Musically, the appeal is not altogether obvious. Not all of it is to my taste. I guess it has more to do with a kinship of spirit. It is not what I consider the world's greatest music, but great it is and—for whatever reason—deeply challenging and personal for me.

Bruckner was kapellmeister at the monastery of St. Augustine in Austria until the age of forty. Although his musical style is quite the opposite of Gregorian, or our English plainchant, he must have absorbed something of the monastic spirit; that must be what particularly attracts me to his work. In his later life in Vienna, he continued to live somewhat like a monk. He never married, composed magnificent symphonies, performed organ concerts, and taught. Gustav Mahler was among his devoted students. Bruckner lived simply and devoutly; he would, for instance, interrupt his classes at the ringing of the Angelus. A 1942 biography titled *Anton Bruckner: Rustic Genius*, by Werner Wolff, conveys the simplicity and even naïveté of this country boy. More than once I heard our late choir director Fr. Chrysogonus say, "Bruckner was as holy as he could be."

This holy, monk-like artist lived in a spirit of detachment; he would humbly consult about his compositions and revise copiously. He died without hearing some of his works performed. The first Bruckner symphony I listened to was the Fifth, one he himself never heard performed by a full orchestra. For that reason the music appealed to me all the more. What first struck me was how architectural the structure was, composed on the grand scale of a great cathedral, suffused with solemnity and sacred air. Some people might find him too ponderous and complex. However, there are many sides to his robust character, and any one of his scherzos will lift you out of your seat; there is no energy quite like it.

During the years I was developing photographs in our darkroom, I listened to Bruckner. Likewise, when on retreat at the hermitage, I always bring Bruckner with me and give a full listening to some symphony. What this amounts to personally is hard to say, but it goes beyond mere musical interest. I often go about kitchen work with his themes running through my mind, or whistling on my lips. His musical meanderings are a hike on an alpine trail with grand views, delicate flowers, runlets along the path, birdcalls; a dark turn past a cliff face opens onto another magnificent vista. All this appeals to a sense of adventure in me; it also brings awareness that God's world is bigger than anyone can measure. One of my high points at the hermitage one year was listening to the ending of the Eighth Symphony while watching a sunset. It equaled the grandeur of the music.

One of my brothers, Br. John, likes him as well, so I'm not Bruckner's only monk-friend in the contemporary world. Monks and nuns easily get this bug about one composer or another. Br. Frederic has listened to the Brahms Requiem a thousand times or so, it seems. Br. Giuseppe cannot listen to Mahler's Second Symphony without his hair standing up and tears coming down. When Fr. Chrysogonus was asked what music is played in heaven, he said Bach. I suspect the reason monks take to a particular classical composition is that it corresponds to some greatness they have experienced, living in the presence of God. It puts into sound what they already know by faith in their lives.

Maybe in heaven the soul connections felt here on earth will prove to be mutual. Could it be that the artist "up there" is pleased to know they have a devoted friend in a monastery down here? I would like to think so; someday there will be mutual enjoyment to be had in this respect. I suspect Bruckner will prove a lot more fun than people might expect.

MONK'S DREAM

Finally, I must make a rather unmonastic confession of a streak of jazz in my ways and days. Monks do not generally take to jazz. For me, it has been a rather short bridge to cross, because of the classical structure and counterpoint of the genre, and for its range and potential of expression. And, yes, I must confess to my own kind of elitism. Well, eventually that will all get leveled out in heaven.

I first took to jazz largely due to the influence of Richard Sisto, whom I met through another notable monastic jazz fan, Fr. Louis, on the day of my final vows. Richard and I have gone on to do a couple of performances combining poetry with drums or piano. The first was at the hermitage for a group of Thomas Merton scholars, who came here for a Sunday Mass and an afternoon sitting on hay bales in the yard, listening to Merton's prose poem "The Early Legend." I also made a piano recording of my poetry with Chuck Marohnic, another Louisville artist. Both of these musicians have a deep affinity with monastic life and an appreciation for the spiritual and liturgical potential of jazz. Chuck has lately released compositions for all one hundred and fifty psalms to be put to use in a liturgical setting. The work took him five years to complete. Richard now prefers to perform in churches or at universities rather than in nightclubs. We have recently been toying with haiku, first read, and then rendered descriptively with drum—a vocabulary of its own.

THOMAS MERTON, NOVICE MASTER

Before I came to the monastery, I spent six weeks in southern New Mexico working on a housing project managed by my brother Max. One evening we drove out to see the desert and to climb a rather singular mountain. It appeared from the distance as a high peak with no others surrounding it. Once we arrived and parked, we began the climb on foot. The mountain no longer appeared so tall; from foot level it seemed undramatic. It was not until we gained elevation, turned, and could see at a great distance that we sensed our real altitude.

Before I left high school, I had read *The Seven Storey Mountain* and had some sense of the stature of Thomas Merton. I had already developed an interest in monastic life, and his autobiography showed me that a modern person, with obvious sophistication and education, could enter a monastery. A monastery appeared to be a place where you could grow in understanding in a spiritually charged community atmosphere. So seemed Gethsemani from afar, but when I arrived and began climbing this monastic mountain for myself, its dry, stony ground no longer seemed quite so exceptional. Not until a month after my interview with the appointed novice master, Fr. Louis, did I learn that this was in fact Thomas Merton. It was a fortunate oversight because by then I had established a relationship with him as a spiritual mentor rather than as a celebrated author.

Not until years later could I look out confidently on the broad landscape that Fr. Louis had opened to my eyes and from that perspective discern my real elevation. The horizon stretches from the medieval Cistercian fathers to Muslim Sufi mystics and modern Hasidic writers, from sacred scripture to contemporary poets like Rainer Maria Rilke and to novelists like William Faulkner. Fr. Louis taught scripture with the kind of literary-analytic skill he most likely learned while studying at Columbia University. His commentaries on the book of Job and the two books of Samuel are most vivid in my mind because he simply traced out the narrative line and drew our interest to what many of us had never paid much attention to.

In his novitiate conferences, Fr. Louis was never very vocal about his views on the political issues he eventually wrote about. He expressed his opinions on racism, disarmament, and other social justice concerns only in the briefest way. He focused on what would be of primary value in a monastic formation and confined his personal interests to his writings. This was to change once he was relieved of his post as novice master. He could turn to his own interests while continuing to teach within the community. His unique social teachings were developed within a contemplative setting, gained from the perspective of the Desert Fathers and from the practice and experience of monastic renunciation. This has proved of true value for me and many others here and abroad.

WHAT WAS HE LIKE?

At this point in my life, it is hard to untangle which strands of spirituality are Fr. Louis's and which are my own. On every side he inspired an attitude of openness, inclusiveness, and integration. He taught from a mind that was open to God and that accepts every person, with a heart willing to penetrate other minds and hearts and to identify with something he found there. This disposition happily brings about an enhancement of one's own experience of life, and that increased experience of life increases empathy for other people.

He and I had a twenty-five-year gap in age, which seemed more like forty years from my point of view as a seventeen-year-old. I was poor at making guesses about a person's age, or you might truthfully say he was old for his age, given his ulcers, digestive problems, and insomnia. Despite these health issues, he displayed vigor at work. I remember him walking with a lilt at the top of the line of novices out to woods or gardens, wearing a straw hat, striding along with a kind of splayed swing of hands and feet that made me think of a healthy cornstalk. In the hayfield he could hoist a bale from the ground up onto a wagon with one sweep. It usually took me four moves—lift, crouch, position, throw.

By the age of forty-three, he had grown a bit rounder and broader in the face compared to early slim-face photographs. His one feature that was most distinctive seems never to have been captured in pictures—his head. The whole head—top and back. There was a power and compactness that emanated, something like a sculpture by Rodin. I would say it was his most prominent feature. The rest of the face was more that of a man of field and forests, like the farmers in Nelson County. And in fact he related to these neighbors very well, as one of their own.

With years, he came to take on the rotund appearance of a benign English don, and I remember how one time he stood watching the young novices passing by and made a fusty utterance: "Most edifying." He must have been putting on a donnish manner from days at Oakham. He enjoyed us novices in spite of our immaturity, insecurity, orneriness, and restlessness. There were about ten or twelve of us in our teens at that time.

Once in choir, when we came to the line in Psalm 119, "How can young people keep their way pure?" he stepped forward and underlined it with his finger. Such was the life of a novice master! When we came to a later line in that psalm—"I understand more than the aged"—his neighbor Fr. Bernard stepped forward and underlined that sentence.

NOVICE BEHAVIOR

At a certain point I decided to grow long sideburns like Elvis Presley, even though our hair was shaved pretty short— sort of a hint of a monastic "greaser" of the 1950s. Fr. Louis looked at me quietly and said, "Disgraceful." I continued to wear them. He came by later and quietly said again, "Disgraceful." Maybe that was the attention I wanted, but before the third "disgraceful" came, I shaved them off. Well, I never liked Elvis Presley anyhow.

At the end of my first season of Lent, I complained that I hadn't improved despite all we'd done. He said there is still Easter season, which is much more powerful.

Even with our age difference, and regardless of my behavior, I always felt Fr. Louis treated me as an equal. His basic attitude toward me bred self-assurance and confidence. Each novice was assigned a session of spiritual direction every other week. The consultation lasted half an hour in his office. The only difference about my particular session, compared to the older novices, was that it often stretched beyond thirty minutes into an hour. At the last minute I would "pull the rabbit out of the hat," as he put it, and continue with some personal matter, and our discussion kept going. It just took me that long to get over shyness and to bring up something serious. Then we would miss Compline, but that never particularly bothered him.

Once I went in to see him, sat down, and he asked me how I was. I said fine, and this and that. Then I asked him how he was. He let out a groan and leaned aside on his hand: "Ohhh!" We laughed, and I asked no further. He later disclosed his dissatisfaction with this form of monastic life: "I have been through this system and got as much out of it as I can, and I need to go on to a more solitary form of life." I hoped he could find it, but I had every intention of pursuing community life as we had it. I admired his love of solitude and meant to develop that myself in this context. I had only a dim idea of how intense the conflict was for him, and later of how he applied to the Vatican for a transition. When that failed and it was all behind him, I learned about it from Fr. Tarcisius, the under-master.

At times it seemed hard to understand ideas he was trying to explain to me, and it took about a year before I could follow his language and his thinking. That was as much a matter of my spiritual immaturity as of my mental limitations. There was much to grow into, and it was good to be stretched and pruned in various ways. Eventually, I could anticipate his next thought because I knew what patterns his reasoning followed. For example, he would mention one word, and then move to its opposite in order to clarify what the first one meant—such as when he distinguished between existential and abstract thinking.

I once told Fr. Louis that at home I had gotten up early and watched *The Today Show* to see the test explosion of a nuclear bomb. His attention narrowed and he asked me if I thought such a thing should be happening in this country. I hesitated. No one had ever asked for my opinion on the matter before. After a quick thought, I said "no." Such was Fr. Louis's approach to the subject—it started by asking a question. Perhaps my "no" was a matter of compliance, but his question made me stop and think carefully about it for myself.

I was once surprised by his show of vulnerability. I went to his office with some kind of game plan of one-upmanship, to make a criticism and then get one back. There were a few monks here who liked to do that, but that was an American style of argument that he never could take to. And basically it was not really my style either, but I was trying it out. When

I started in, he didn't reply and appeared sensitive. Later, our abbot Dom James instructed me not to say anything that would offend people. I was too dense to know I ever did.

WORDS OF WISDOM

In talk among the novices, I had heard mention of Zen here and there, so once I went to Fr. Louis's door to ask what Zen is. He took that as very funny and answered by grabbing a book and pretending to bop me on the head. That was his peculiar answer. When I persisted, he said Zen is, "There is a cherry tree outside the window." His answer pertained to direct experience, but it was too much for my puzzled brain to get right away.

If a novice showed interest in other spiritual traditions and practices, he might get a few leads. For instance, I found a novice standing on his head behind a hedge and was told he was practicing yoga. Fr. Louis did some of that himself, but I never saw it.

To many, it might sound surprising that he never gave any group instruction in meditation at all. I believe his assumption was that our common life of lectio divina, prayer, silence, and choir were enough to eventually lead to meditation. There is no Cistercian tradition about the practice of meditation. The community atmosphere and observances suffice for fostering results. This is best summarized in Fr. Louis's own words in a letter to Etta Gullick, a scholar at Oxford:

> I must say there is a good proportion of contemplative prayer in the novitiate. I don't use special methods. I try to make them love the freedom and peace of being with God alone in faith and simplicity, to abolish all divisiveness and diminish all useless strain and concentration on one's own efforts and all formalism: all the nonsense of taking seriously the apparatus of an official

prayer life, in the wrong way (but to love liturgy in simple faith as the place of Christ's sanctifying presence in the community).

One time I asked him about another word I heard him use that was new to me: *existentialism*. I wanted to hear some clarification. He said it had to do with knowledge through personal experience. That did not seem definite and I wanted an example. He grabbed the Bible and read from Psalm 107 such vivid lines:

> Some went down to the sea in ships, doing business on the mighty waters;
> they saw the deeds of the Lord, his wondrous works in the deep.
> For he commanded and raised the stormy wind, which lifted up the waves of the sea.
> They mounted up to heaven, they went down to the depths;
> their courage melted away in their calamity;
> they reeled and staggered like drunkards . . .
> Then they cried to the Lord in their trouble . . .
> he made the storm be still . . .
> Let them thank the Lord for his steadfast love.

I had no idea we were hearing from existentialists every day in the psalms—a philosophy as old as that!

I heard Fr. Louis gave Rorschach tests, and I asked if he would do that for me. These were inkblots that suggested something in the subconscious. He showed reluctance, but with my coaxing we brought them out of the desk. His analysis of me was that I hold things back and keep them within. I knew that was true, and still do that to some extent. He said the problem today is not that people suppress the sexual instinct, as Freud said; now, people suppress the spiritual self and keep it repressed.

About a year into my novitiate, I had heard enough sermons about monks and being a monk. I went to his door and said, "I want to become a monk." He said, "Good." Simple words for simple things—simple but life-giving things.

As a spiritual director, Fr. Louis seemed to be mostly nondirective. I expected something more from him, but what I got was space to breathe, to be myself, and to develop at my own pace. Occasionally he pointed out what he saw in me, something I could not see but that from the outside was quite apparent. For instance, as I grew more confident and familiar with the community, I allowed myself what I thought was spontaneity. This seemed all right to me, but he remarked that my way of being spontaneous was compulsive. I thought I was just being free and open, but that remark caused me to realize I needed to calm down, relax, and be at peace.

Often his way of offering a correction was indirect. He would describe how someone was in the habit of thinking or acting, some third party, left unnamed. I might guess who it was, but the real point was not about somebody else but about me. It served as a word of caution meant to bring me back to myself to discern where it pertained.

One time he asked me, "How do you know God loves you?" I fumbled out some vague reply. He said, "You know God loves you because he brought you here and takes care of you."

Spiritual Directing

There was in Fr. Louis an enormous capacity for nonverbal communication. It might even have dwarfed his great capacity for verbal communication. I never tried to plumb his more subtle depths since it frightened me. He seemed to be able to discern a lot just by looking at you, all so quick and personal that I was thrown off guard. This might have been what the Desert Fathers called "practicing discernment of spirits." I wanted to retreat to words where I could feel in control, and he told me as much. I was unaware of how guarded I was by habit.

One morning during the first spring season I was at Gethsemani, I went outside to the high overlook above "the bottoms," a word commonly used here for a valley. The sky was incredibly blue, and everything was exquisitely fresh. My senses were cleansed by the rigor of our life, and intensified by my budding manhood. Everything in that quiet moment was more vivid than I had ever sensed before.

I strolled around the corner and met Fr. Louis, who saw immediately my happy state and looked pleased. When I saw that he saw, I became self-conscious. He detected the barrier I had thrown up, and his look turned dark. For me it was a moment in which I felt too obvious. Later he complained of my being self-conscious. Why didn't I just say how happy I was and let him hear that? In fact, I felt little confidence embarking upon the shores of communication when I was unsure of saying anything right. And I was not sure I wanted to be so easy to read.

A day after our encounter, he told me I was narcissistic. That was a heck of a big word for me, and he proceeded to recount the myth of Narcissus—a young man who resisted relationships with others but fell in love with his own image in a pond. He said I was always looking at myself; I wanted to be spiritually beautiful. I was looking at myself in choir, in prayer, and that accounted for the "chafing sensation" that I complained about. I was too turned inward on myself and consequently felt sour and cramped within. He said that was narcissism and added that most young men are narcissistic. His general remedy was to live the life here at the monastery, stop looking at myself, and forget myself. That counsel remains until today a code of my monastic life.

He returned to this advice later in my novitiate when he said this was an easy life, and if you just go through the day and do your work and follow choir and the observances, growth would happen. It was a simple approach and explains why he was mostly nondirective. He believed the Holy Spirit took care of the hidden growth of the novice.

But there was a point later where this sane advice needed to be balanced by a period of developing self-knowledge. This found its moment a few years after I finished the novitiate. I eventually came under the care of Fr. John Eudes Bamberger, who became my master of juniors a few years before my solemn profession in 1968. That too—the search for self-knowledge—remains a core code of my life, and blending these two together is what really makes up my inner discipline. The balancing pivots on trusting my self to God in whatever act I am to do, or whatever interaction arises with another person or group. Sometimes, but not always, that means an explicit prayer, but never without an implicit understanding that nothing is all about me. Yet nothing can be authentic unless it comes from openness to the moment for what it might bring.

Fr. Louis himself proved to be a master of introspection, but it came at a cost. I believe he had to battle narcissism all his life. For me, nothing of this freedom from self-absorption came easily, given my inclination to guilt, self-doubt, insecurity, and secrecy. What I know of freedom comes from living in the Spirit with confidence in God's largeness of heart and mercy.

THE NOVITIATE

Our group of novices comprised a wide range of nationalities, professions, and ages—including doctors, lawyers, Canadians, and Latin Americans. Fr. Louis loved to repeat a remark by one tall, lanky lawyer who had to hear out his novice master's complaints about people and the monastery, and replied, "Well, Father, to each his own." Fr. Louis was bemused at the good sense. Another novice had recently graduated valedictorian at a prominent Catholic university and found himself thwarted by Fr. Louis in his efforts to get attention. He soon left the novitiate. Fr. Louis was wary of anyone trying to draw attention to himself. Perhaps that was because he could see that it had once been a fault of his own and perhaps still was.

One short, middle-aged man in our group who seldom spoke, Br. Lawrence, left and was to emerge on the world scene as Ernesto Cardenal, an influential poet and member of the cabinet in the Sandinista administration in Nicaragua. Ernesto made very simple sculptures out of concrete or plaster, and while here he wrote the shortest and most pithy poems of his career. His later style was epic and expansive. Frater Lawrence loved to tease the young novices but often gave me the impression of being very intense and inward, and was at times feeling anguish. Another novice, a rather formidable black man, later in life emerged as president of New York City's Hostos Community College. Another, who had been in the air force, eventually became president of a "multiversity," as he called it, in Illinois. Another one, even younger than me, left and became a brain surgeon and head of a large clinic in Louisville. One of the most soft-spoken young monks of all emerged as James Finley, prominently known today as a spiritual teacher, author, psychologist, and lecturer on Merton. Someone who entered the novitiate a month after me eventually became my abbot in 1973, Fr. Timothy Kelly. I occasionally remind him that I am his senior in religious life. Another, a priest in his forties, had been a Divine Word missionary in New Guinea. After he made his profession, his outstanding homilies were collected and published. Thousands know him as Fr. Matthew Kelty. Gethsemani had many remarkable men, but I only mention those in particular who were with me in the novitiate, and leave out individuals who were before or after my time there.

I could always tell when Fr. Matthew and Fr. Louis were engaged in spiritual direction. There would be laughter roaring through the office window. My own sessions were usually quiet and serious. Those two jovial priests seemed too sheltered from my kind of doubts about the Church—papal infallibility, transubstantiation, and now-obsolete notions of "no salvation outside of the Church." I was inward and preoccupied. I mistrusted this religious environment where doubt, I assumed, was held in abeyance. I assumed Fr. Louis, as a convert, struggled with doubts in his day, but he seemed unconcerned with them now in the way that I was.

Eventually I was to find that he struggled with doubts continually but had integrated them as an essential in the true life of faith. However, in my discussions with him, my simmering doubts were never answered to my satisfaction. This was not due to his neglect so much as to the fact that in his view answers were beside the point. The real issue was the struggle with God. Faith, he said, is like Jacob wrestling in the night with something he cannot name. Faith means to be that much engaged with God. Doubt is a part of faith, not something to be excluded. Without doubt there may be no real engagement at all, just a placid piety that masks as faith but is simply an evasion. Doubt is sometimes the fruit of love, a love that seems thwarted.

For my confessor I was recommended to Fr. Augustine Wolfe, who was quite willing to discuss at length my thoughts and problems with Church teachings. And eventually Vatican II clarified many things that were worrisome to me. My studies in theology later gave a better perspective.

Fr. Louis had certain reservations about people who study theology thinking it will get them closer to God. He said it quite possibly could take you further away from God. He had a distaste for the neo-Scholastic style where "everything is cut and dried, all laid out, A-B-C and Bam—you come to a conclusion," as he put it. His interest was experience-based theology that retains the sense of mystery.

MY FAMILY

Once Fr. Louis asked about my relationship to my mother (my father had died eight years previously), and I made a caustic remark that I would save her if she were drowning. He was set aback a bit, but probably sensed this attempt at cleverness was a cover-up for my inability to articulate what the relationship really was. He replied that his own mother did not like him. That suddenly struck me as far worse than anything I had to complain about. I always knew my mother loved me, but could not really appreciate it. I just took it for granted. Doubt about that never crossed my mind, but little did I know at the time how precious that basic love is.

Something more to the foreground of my mind in those days was the interest and love that my older sister, Carolyn, showed to me. We began to have personal conversations when she returned home from college in Cleveland. She asked questions like, What is humility? We shared a love of classical music and books, and she gave me *The Brothers Karamazov*, by Dostoevsky. That kind of attention was a new sort of love for me, and I think it opened, in part, a new capacity for reflection and a capacity to love God. Strangely, the novel gave me an example of a young man like myself—youngest of three grown brothers—who entered a monastery and found there a saintly starets, Abba Zossima. This proved to be a preview of the months ahead for me, and in ways neither of us could have expected—rather to her chagrin, but to me a joyous wonder.

Fr. Louis took a special interest in Carolyn and made a point of visiting with her when the family came, because she had recently left the Church. He believed she was a very spiritual person, and he found her honest and straightforward. I saw the two of them sitting on a wall at the far end of the avenue, with Carolyn kicking her feet. He later wrote of how forthright she was, but little of substance evidently came of the meeting. Fr. Louis wrote at length in his private journal about their visit—something I was not to read until decades later.

Carolyn had been critical of my leaving the "real" world, burying my talents, and entering a monastery. She shared no belief in the value of prayer. After her visit with Fr. Louis, she continued to send me her "blasts" as she called them, and said contemplation is just a "spiritual orgasm." When I showed one such letter to Fr. Louis, he said the remarks were aimed at him. Although a new idea to me, I took it as a real possibility. As a result of his comment, something changed. It was no longer I alone that bore the brunt of these charges, at least not to such an extent. That shifted the burden of the whole matter, and I ceased to be so reactive. This new perspective cleared my preoccupied thoughts for more immediate concerns in my daily life. I stopped writing letters in my head, standing at the back of choir while the priests in the sanctuary were waiting for the incensor that I was supposed to bring at the offertory. Things had gotten that bad.

One of the most enduring counsels Fr. Louis gave me concerned my three brothers and older sister who had left the Church. My twin sister, Eileen, eventually followed suit, and I worried how I could fix all that. Little results came of what they dubbed "The Epistles of Br. Paul." Fr. Louis assured me in a quiet tone of sincere faith that "they are in God's hands." That simple observation changed my attitude and has stayed with me over the decades. With time, the whole family came to appreciate the unique value the contemplative life holds for the world; they accepted me and enjoyed being here for visits, and brought their growing crop of children to the lively reunions at our family guesthouse. My nieces and nephew, as adults, retain fond memories of those many happy gatherings. I have long abandoned efforts to change any of them. They are good people, and maybe there is some strange order in the balance of things that remains invisible. Before Cain slew Abel the Lord told him, "If you do well, will you not be accepted?" (Gn 4:7). Perhaps this indicates some theological basis for secularism.

PREPARING FOR VOWS

As a novice, I had ongoing doubts about my ability to persevere here over a lifetime. It was a frequent but not constant bother because there was another, more frightening concern. It was not very clear in those years before the Cuban Missile Crisis that any of us would be left alive in the near future. The threat of nuclear war seemed so persistent that it haunted my dreams. Apart from that, the thought seemed incredible that I would still be in the monastery if I lived into my seventies. And here I still am, closing in on eighty! It still seems incredible. At some point Fr. Louis told me that, if I persevere, my life would be unique. And unique it has been. The sense never left me—something like an intuition of faith—that I should continue through it all, leading this life, trusting in the Lord and leaving it to God to take care of the next thing to come, whatever that may be. God forbid, however, if anyone should take me as a typical monk or as at all exemplary. Everyone has to pick a path through the stickers and briars and come out the other side in his own way. Maybe being unique was part of the appeal to me. At least Fr. Louis's remark made it possible for me to accept that my life would be unique. Otherwise, my life would have developed in accord with my preconceived expectations rather than as it has, gradually emerged from the hand of God.

When it came time to take my first vows, Fr. Louis said something that has been reinforced for me over the years. He told me how he personally thought I indeed had a vocation, and would not recommend me for vows if he did not think so. He said that he owed it specifically to me, to my mother, to Carolyn, and the rest of the family to see that I was making the right decision. This was an expression of respect and love that I can look back on as genuine and lasting. Perhaps without my knowing it, those words carried me through rough patches. It was not one of those things I ever much reflected on, but it had its lasting effect without my recognizing it clearly until now.

Part of the ritual of profession is to write out the vows on a sheet of vellum. I was so clumsy and hasty about it all that I filled the page before I reached the end of the vows and had to continue on the back side. When I showed the page to Fr. Louis, he expressed some chagrin but did not ask me to rewrite it.

After vows, as I prepared to leave the novitiate, Fr. Louis predicted that I would be "at sea" once I was on the professed monks' side of the monastery. He was willing to let me stay on longer in the novitiate, but I was eager to move over to live with the rest of the community, which had a different scriptorium and grand parlor and dormitory. But sure enough, I was at sea. I did not have as much confidence in the spiritual directors and was in a larger group of priests and scholastics whom I did not know very well. Still, I had no regrets because I could not rely indefinitely on Fr. Louis and wanted to launch out into the wider community.

Since then, I have sailed far and wide, spiritually speaking, but all in view of the lighthouse long left behind. In one way or another, Fr. Louis continues to be a mentor to me, through books, discussions, and friendships.

In that regard I am not unique. I know of countless people who go through life with a continuous connection to his writings and influence. For me it was partly circumstantial, partly by choice. As his unpublished manuscripts appeared in print, I read them, and the earliest studies of Merton scholars were helpful, but the sheer volume of new books soon became overwhelming and the output continues yearly.

HELPING THE LEGACY

During the years I was still in temporary vows, I was given the job of operating the mimeograph machine. That mostly meant running off stencils given me by Fr. Louis for his class notes, essays, and later for his *Cold War Letters* focused on nuclear proliferation and civil rights. Thus I was privy to the ongoing development of his thinking, and I lived in the grip of the tension this created with authorities in our order. In effect, you could say I was his underground publisher since some of those topics had been forbidden by the abbot general for wider publication. Fr. Louis was dealing with serious and urgent global issues, and Dom Gabriel Sortais deemed it unsuitable for monks to get involved in such matters.

About that time a new job was given me as assistant to our very competent electronics man, Br. Kilian. He conceived the notion of recording Fr. Louis's talks in the novitiate and playing them the next morning to the lay brothers in the "potato room," where vegetables were prepared daily for dinner. I could not attend those novitiate conferences since I was no longer a novice, but I could listen to the tapes—and eventually over six hundred recordings were made, at the press of my finger on the starter button.

When the general chapter of the Cistercians decided on the unification of the order, there was no longer a division between the lay brothers and the choir monks. The life of the brothers was mainly devoted to manual labor; they did not participate in the Latin Office. The choir monks were focused on liturgy, sang the Office, and had a sung Mass every day, as well as private Mass. These scholastics followed a course of studies mainly directed to priestly ordination. After the unification, Fr. Louis's conferences were opened to anyone in monastic formation, and later to anyone who wanted to attend. My focus shifted from priestly studies to monastic studies. I, and several other choir monks, rebelled against the idea that a choir monk has to become a priest. Study of monastic history demonstrated that the monastic vocation was a lay vocation. Priesthood is secondary and nonessential. To this day, I remain un-ordained yet dedicated to choir and study.

As Fr. Louis eventually became free of his job as novice master in 1965 and moved on to the hermitage full time, he continued to give talks and expanded them into areas of more personal interest to him: on writers like T. S. Eliot, William Faulkner, Edwin Muir, and Rilke; and on traditions such as mystical Hasidism and Sufism. Strange to say, he presented no series on Buddhism—that interest was close to him but not, as he gauged it, to the other monks.

Soon after Fr. Louis's death, I began making copies of these tapes to mail to other monasteries. The Merton Literary Trust soon took over their dissemination, and Electronic Paperbacks began to publish them. The first tapes to which I directed the trustees were the talks on Sufism, which I thought to be the most extraordinary. Today there are CDs on a multitude of topics available from the current distributor, Now You Know Media.

For the last thirty years I have enjoyed involvement with the International Thomas Merton Society, and I have been on its board of directors several times. I was part of the Thomas Merton Foundation from its inception and continued into its evolution as the Thomas Merton Institute, until its eventual demise. Since 1971, there has been a monthly Merton Circle that meets here at the abbey; core members have been professors from the University of Kentucky, philosophers, scholars, some neighbors, doctors, a power company manager, a Jewish scholar—many very ordinary and extraordinary men and women attending over nearly five decades. This regularly brings my attention back to the writings and engagement in ongoing discussions about Fr. Louis and his thinking. In all of these ways, I continue to be happy to immerse myself in the deep waters of his wisdom.

Nature, My Guru

I am in the rigorous habit of sitting outdoors for prayer and meditation.

This is partly a matter of principle, partly a preference, and sometimes simply practical. For one thing, I can stay awake more easily. For me, the church is too warm and comfortable. Meditating in my cell, likewise, I feel too confined unless I face an open window. I remain outdoors whatever the climate: hot, cold, or clement. When it's rainy, I'm in a nook under an overhanging roof. It looks across a small plateau of graves marked by white crosses, standing like children with hands spread wide in greeting. Beyond are wooded knobs.

> Lowing clouds roll down
> ridge to thick carpet of woods—
> Luxurious greens.

Schola Natura

I take Mother Nature as my spiritual teacher, tough and gentle. I stay at her feet through each year's long, twelve-month lesson. Severe days are as important as mild, the drab as much as the glamorous. Each year is a course taken with nothing omitted, dropped, or skipped—no choosing and picking. If the temperature is four above zero, I'm out there for the usual thirty-minute session. Sometimes this calls for endurance, but no more than what a farmer tending the cows' needs, or a daily commuter waiting for a bus.

41

One day may be Eden, another a dim limbo. Each mood molds my soul to its profile. I am governed and made into something larger than myself. One morning appears as a Chinese painting with cloaks of fog concealing here, parting there, revealing hills, trees, and fields. Another morn displays a brilliant sprawl of clarity, the color too good to be true, unbearably perfect, until the sun heightens and the sky blanches into midday heat.

When I first arrived at the monastery, the guestmaster told me that the contemplative life is not a matter of sitting under a shade tree. The good priest had a point, no doubt, but eventually he left the community and I am still here sitting under shade trees. I can't understand why more of the monks don't do that. To me, it is nourishment for the soul. The humors stir, enzymes form, hormones shift; energy rises from the ground, a life field gathers. I thrive a happy animal and blossom. Why not enjoy something given so freely for all?

I like what Fr. Louis wrote in his poem "O Sweet Irrational Worship": "I am earth, earth," and "By ceasing to question the sun / I have become light." Such should be a part of every life; there is nothing special to be made of it, rather to be made something of—that is what I allow. I love the lines Wendell Berry wrote, in number seven of his fine *Sabbath* poems, about a place you can go that is quiet, and why it is quiet, because from long use and familiarity such places "are themselves / your thoughts."

DISCIPLINARY PRACTICE

The rigors and rewards of being present to days and nights are worth it. Trust and perseverance are the price. Submission, confidence, resolution, and a taste for joy are the reward. Moreover, it must be a choice. Fr. Matthew Kelty in *Flute Solo* wrote that while other monks are coming in from the rain, he is putting on his raincoat and heading out. I ask, in addition, why the raincoat?

When I cannot go out in the weather, I do what I can to bring it in. My window remains open when I sit and read, whether summer or winter. If need be, I'll wrap up in a blanket and wear a cap and turn off the thermostat so as not to waste fuel. Inviting in the fresh air makes me feel more alive, and with sufficient clothing there is no need to get chilled, even while sitting very still over a book. The body generates its own pocket of warmth inside a blanket, as well as inside our Cistercian habit, which is a single garment from ankle to neck.

During summer, with no screen on the window at night, having a solitary lamp on my desk, I receive a small array of flying visitors that provide occasional amusement. Certain moths, not the gray ones, display elegant designs. Moths are underrated, favor going to their butterfly cousins. However, a smart clothing designer could make a fortune by imitating the subtle shades and patterns of certain moths. Mosquitoes are generally no nuisance until September after the cliff swallows and purple martins depart. These efficiently devour most of the mosquitoes while in residence. For protection from these pests, lemongrass or a lotion by Avon is effective, lasting long through night into morning.

No Lasting Place

My favorite meditation locations have changed over the years. St. John of the Cross advised against getting attached to a particular place of meditation. Yet I find that I stay addicted to one or two spots for as long as two or three years at a stretch. Recently, one such spot was atop a retaining wall, with a thirty-foot drop. It had an expansive view of the valley and the rising sun. I pointed out that height where I sit to my friend Richard Sisto, and he said I had done that before. I took him to mean I had meditated there in a previous incarnation. While I claim no knowledge about that, I have little doubt that a high cave on a cliff in Mesopotamia would be much to my liking. I lately had to relinquish my sublime perch because a fence was put up. Someone must have grown nervous that I would doze off and fall over the edge. Even if I went to sleep there, a fall was not really possible. Besides, I like to feel a tinge of vertigo precisely to keep me awake. The fence is of a clever, minimalistic design with five horizontal wires that do not obstruct the view. Should I want to, I could easily roll under the bottom wire and sit as previously. Instead, I took all this as a sign to migrate elsewhere.

These changing locations become inaccessible on their own accord. On the sunrise corner of that same retaining wall, I once stood years ago and attended to the changing sky and shifting hues of the foggy fields and forest. Since then a juniper bush has grown dramatically, spread, and blocked access. The juniper branches spill down the cliff side in a green cascade. Who knows, but in a few years it may reach another fifteen feet to the ground. One nice thing about living a long time in one location is watching the trees and shrubs slowly grow year to year.

Come to think of it, I did in fact favor such high outlooks before—in a previous existence, if you consider fifty-eight years ago, my novitiate days, an earlier incarnation. There was once a narrow platform abutting another retaining wall (we have three terraces) off to the side of twelve descending steps from the upper to the lower garden. One could read at leisure there, view the comings and goings of novices, and smell and watch pigs in the bottoms.

My early childhood home in West Virginia was located on Outlook Road, which may well have foreshadowed my course in life. It was a place to look out from. You might say it fixed me in a mindset. The word *contemplation* in Greek is *theorien*: "to look." Our front door opened on a concrete stoop with no railings, raised about six feet above the yard, with side steps plunging down the hillside to the driveway. It seemed a scary place for a child—or for a mother with small twins (my sister Eileen and me)—although it never bothered me much, once I learned to be careful. One of my favorite passages from St. Gregory of Nyssa is his description of contemplation as coming to the edge of an abyss and looking down. One day Fr. Louis described how we are all sitting atop a volcano and don't even know the danger below. This metaphor implicitly suggests the depths, which was his preferred image. Depths are hidden and dark.

I, too, prefer depth, but depth I can stand above, like a valley spread out and streaked with morning sunrays. One of the agreeable aspects of the site of Fr. Louis's hermitage is that, while it verges on no steep incline, it looks out across a distant valley to the broad Muldraugh escarpment some twenty miles away. Late afternoon sun heightens the soft contours of the far wooded slopes stretching east to west— where our old abbot, Dom James Fox, had his own hermitage located, lost somewhere far up Coon Hollow Road. Lately this idyllic rustic view has been punctured by a blinking cell-phone tower facing me. That surely would have made Fr. Louis storm off to Alaska in indignation, but the rest of us have to live with it.

For the past few years, after Mass, I have walked four minutes to the lumber shed, which overlooks a lake, the woods, and the long enclosure wall gracefully flowing along the contours of the land. That wall marks a boundary between the inside and outside of the monastic enclosure area. It was erected in the 1930s when people rode or walked right up to the monastery; a physical separation needed to be established, and the long stretch of the wall encircles hundreds of acres around us. Our wall is less functional today, more symbolic and evocative of every ancient monastic location where sacred presence has been planted in the wilderness. I have seen no one walk that stretch of wall or that field in years. For that reason it seems like untrodden ground, all the more privileged to the divine—and to the roaming deer.

I once explored all of this in a poem, "Restless Silence":

> The enclosure wall runs the field,
> ducks behind some pines
> skirts the forest, dips and rises,
> gently drops, then disappears.
>
> Beyond, I can hear snow
> melting in the woods.
>
> What am I waiting for?
> What enlightenment is in the sun
> reflecting off the icy lake,
> wearing it to a thin slick?
>
> Dry grass in the wet field
> is dusty with sunlight.
> What is the grass waiting for?
> A pigeon leaves a tree for another tree.
>
> I can hear the sun
> grazing the dusty grass,
> until a breeze interrupts briefly
> then settles for . . . a something . . .
>
> Was it here already and gone?
> Or was it only here
> so I would come and wait?

Trees recently began growing inside as well as outside the long wall, and soon the whole edifice will disappear into a growth of forest. Roots will undermine the foundation, and eventually it will crumble as rain makes the ground shift, such as it already has on a twenty-yard stretch, allowing the wind to blow it down.

Walking meditation is provided by the graveyard and sidewalks curving around the back of the church. Death and life are visible there. It can't be avoided. I see it every day. One need not consciously reflect on death; it is there as part of our grounds, and you live with it. Occasionally I used to see an older monk, the late Br. Martin, leaning on the railing and gazing down into the lower level where his old friends are buried, those he worked with during his years as the community plumber. The aging human body gradually leans forward, closer to the earth, as if gravity were pulling it toward its destiny. St. Benedict accredited that lowered head to a monk's growth in humility. I hope that is true, but meanwhile I am trying to practice good posture and humility as well.

EMINENT TREES I HAVE KNOWN

Several of the esteemed doctors and masters of my spiritual formation have been trees. Trees have often touched and molded my life of meditation. At one time, two linden trees were my companions, one on either side, where I sat and faced sunrise. A day came when construction of the new infirmary required their elimination. I watched from a distance as they were plowed over with a bulldozer, and the sight provoked my voice to a high, soft pitch. Such feelings of kinship were a surprise to me; I had never made that sound before, yet it seemed the only decent thing to do at the moment—to lift my voice in empathy. I later learned some African tribes use that "keening" in funeral ceremonies.

At another time, destruction of a chokeberry tree provoked a response. In those years I would sit silently on cinder blocks by the lumber shed, shaded by this crabbed, gnarled chokeberry, one of a kind on our extensive grounds, a character with cantankerous features, ragged bark, and angular branches. Birds favored it for its tough, dry berries. I arrived there one evening to find the corpse of this chokeberry pushed down the slope. I had received warnings that it would soon happen, to allow propane trucks to pass by. This time, instead of seething with indignation, I let the chokeberry go as I would a beloved friend.

Jonathan Montaldo, a friend and Merton scholar, was visiting at that time with some friends. One was trained in Native American ritual. He provided a liturgy to contain the feeling and still my swell of anger. Four of us gathered on the site where the tree lay prostrate. We sat in a circle and discussed my kinship with the tree, how things might have been done differently, what might replace it. Incense was offered in the four directions, with thoughts on what each direction meant. Then came a "smudging," a blend of sage, pine, and tobacco on a bark tray. The smudging honored the tree, and all trees that sustain our life with fresh oxygen, beauty, and presence. In a short time, a red cedar, long overshadowed by the chokeberry, grew rapidly and began to provide cooling shade better than any before.

Preeminent among the master trees is an awesome ginkgo, with a massive trunk that is eighteen feet three inches in diameter. It stands in our front garden, and the shade is dense. Branches rise in muscular sinews, spreading out, becoming long and thick. Once you draw near and stand by, the air turns primordial and the feeling is of another world in ancient times. As a species, the ginkgo is 55 million years old and once covered North America and Siberia. The Ice Age diminished its population, but it survived in China. This venerable survivor came as a sapling directly from China in the hands of Dom Edmond Obrecht. Dom Edmond was Gethsemani's third abbot, who came from Belgium and had a European flair for collecting art and artifacts, bringing them home from his many travels on behalf of the order.

I knew of no such tree in West Virginia, but before I entered the monastery I saw a movie that ended with a troubled young man running through the night to a secret place in the forest where he could find solace. The next scene opened on a morning when he was asleep, sprawled under a huge tree raining down golden leaves upon him. I had no idea that this monastery in Kentucky would have exactly that kind of tree and that I would behold this golden downpour every autumn. It has been a solace to me and many others. The tree retains its host of brilliant yellow leaves until the first hard frost, and then showers down the whole bank before morning is ended. A wonder to every novice who enters and stays here.

The leaf of the *Ginkgo biloba* is famous for its benefits for the brain. It would not be surprising to see Bilbo Baggins or a hobbit resting in its branches. The magical globe of this druid suggests something out of *The Lord of the Rings*.

I climbed the ginkgo once with a young woman who specializes in herbs and edibles of the forest. We harvested leaves into paper bags, and she juiced them for health purposes. The juice squeezed from the leaves has a lemony taste. I took it for a year but was not clever enough to tell if I was any smarter.

In our community archives is a black-and-white, 8 mm film of Fr. Louis on the day of his priestly ordination in 1949. He sat on a bench under this tree talking to his friends. The film is silent, but the vigorous sweep of his hands bespeaks an active, enthusiastic mind. He was thirty-four years old, and his companions that day were Robert Lax, James Laughlin, and Dan Walsh, among others.

This tall, massive presence wonderfully nourishes conversations between visitors and monks, and engenders wisdom. The Buddha was enlightened under a Bodhi tree, a kindred species, but the Bodhi displays a more evolved, complex leaf pattern compared to the simple, straight fan lines of the ginkgo leaf. One large, low branch has begun probing down an extension to eventually reach the ground and take root, where it will thicken into an additional supporting trunk. I notice a few extra inches of length every year.

The life of my giant, green predecessor has worked its way through my body. Where prayer is practiced, where meditation is a matter of being present, everything present is included and embraces the mind and soul. These places "are themselves / your thoughts."

INSTRUCTED BY CHANGE

With all this immersion in sense objects, what about "the dark night of the senses"—what the Spanish mystics designate an essential stage of spiritual progress? Specifically, such progress brings detachment from the senses in order to free the heart for what is inward and beyond sense. No doubt, this is required to become centered and reoriented. There are times when closing the eyes and dwelling in the heart is sufficient, true, and necessary. But often, after a stretch of meditation, I find the voice of a bird or the sweep of the wind invites me and reminds me that bliss in life is not all mine. Detachment from sense and from particular objects, paradoxically, frees my mind to become acutely aware of what nature and the senses have to tell me; I become attuned to my body in a deeper way.

Nature itself cultivates detachment by its very destructibility. Change is intrinsic to matter; I can simply slow down and witness change as a lesson in life. There is small chance of attachment where nothing long endures. The face of the most idyllic mornings fades. Even the sheer paradise of a Kentucky spring leaves me dissatisfied. The heart instinctively knows this is not sufficient. It chafes for something more.

To call it "desolation" may be too dramatic. Wonders of the world declare, "We are not enough." The best I can do is to take things as they are and leave them at that. The changing day and the daily community schedule reinforce this natural training. Being ordinary is a way to be true. To get up at the call of the bell to choir means I release one thing and prepare myself for another. Such change comes as a relief as much as a demand, and again, to leave choir and go to work is a relief. The monastic day provides a rhythm of change, a continual releasing, taking hold, and releasing. It is an exercise in detachment. Through it all I lose myself because I am not always in control, making the decisions; even ideas of my spiritual progress fall by the wayside in behalf of the matter at hand. Could it be as simple as this, what Jesus meant when he said, "The kingdom of heaven is at hand"?

LIVING AT THE NATURAL PACE

A friend once said, "I would love to get inside the head of a monk to see what your life is like." I doubt anyone would want to stay inside my head for very long. Not much appears there in terms of spiritual excitement, let alone progress. At most, I live with a dim intuition, an implicit faith that something worthwhile is going on. That does not usually prove very interesting to me, let alone to other people. Yet it is of irreducible value. I like the lines of Emily Dickinson:

> Growth of Man — like Growth of Nature,
> Gravitates within.
> Atmosphere, and sun endorse it —
> But it stir — alone.
>
> Each its difficult Ideal
> Must achieve — Itself —
> Through the solitary prowess
> Of a silent life.

That is about as fine an expression of good old Trappist spirituality as I can imagine. It has the tone and grit of how Dom James Fox preached in his chapter talks on perseverance. He sometimes used the same word my mother used: "stick-to-it-iveness." I was lucky to learn that word early in life. Dom James was the abbot for my first ten years in the monastery. He certainly practiced what he preached, and perhaps overdid it at times. Today we could use more of the virtue of this vice.

At least it is a vice if taken for raw willpower. As a virtue, it is a natural instinct bequeathed by nature itself. It is a yielding to life, to the Spirit operating in a hidden, undramatic way, and to the operation of grace. Even though nothing appears to be happening, something is. It means long, patient abiding in the poverty of the present moment, without making great claims concerning it. Something much bigger, indeed, is at work all the time. To take stock and measure it is to diminish it. To define it yields a fiction—it cannot be objectified. At best, I may name it, rather than define it, since a name comes closer to mystery, for who knows what is in a name?

Time, as I bear it daily, is weighted with eternity. The God who resists being named has a name for me. Throughout my time on earth, every day is a letter in the spelling out of that name for me: a slow revelation of who I am. It is a name that cannot be pronounced until the end of life. That pronunciation, I suggest, is what is meant by "the judgment." Judgment is the clarification and truth of each person. *I am.*

I am what I live. Don't tell me who I am yet. It is still being spelled out.

A WEEK AT THE HERMITAGE

Moonlight awakened me from sleep on the porch of the hermitage. The high moon enhanced the trees with vertical light accentuating lines of the tall trunks. This quiet assembly stood as elegant aristocrats, softly drenched in descending, silvery gauze of courtesy and graciousness.

Nearby, a lone cricket kept careful track of all this while a distant, sustained note spread widely over the fields. This late August coolness has silenced nightly katydids who can rack and vibrate the air from all sides, especially in this close grove, or what is slowly crowding into one. Years ago this yard opened to the sky, with hardy saplings planted to become the sheltering presences they are today.

SETTLING IN

I came here for a week of retreat after a loud morning of heat and bother in the kitchen, of pressure and song at Mass with the community and Sunday crowd. After packing in and setting up, I sat on the chair marked "the Bench of Dreams" and got over my life, with eyes closed, wanting nothing but to be stayed interiorly within what stays you.

Stillness lasted about an hour, and finally my reopened eyes showed the afternoon had gathered to shades of evening. Time moves, and I am moved along. But here there is no urgency to get to the next thing. I pursue no schedule except one of my own devising. I decided to push Vespers back an hour. To be free of a schedule looks attractive, but to have no schedule at all can be as obsessive as having one too rigid. Total freedom leaves me wondering what to do next. I forget that question if I allow the sun to determine my actions.

I would do well to have more of the spirit of the late Br. Harold of fond memory—my peer in the novitiate. He had what might be called "the gift of leisure." During this hour of my staying, something of Harold's face moved close and merged with mine. It felt good company, and I don't know why I thought of him after so many years since his death. I guess I needed it. There was something imperturbable about Harold, and he was a natural for the Buddhism he was long interested in. If there is an aristocracy of souls, he would be toasted in their gentle company.

Harold remained serene even as he gradually slipped into dementia, and I will always remember him sitting contentedly under the cherry tree, with blossoms falling around and upon his head, he not bothering to brush them off. From the hermitage I later heard a saw roaring and soon discovered they had cut down that very tree Harold sat under. It was dying, withered by deep winter freezes. Not far off was a Washington cherry, also slowly dying, planted sideways at a steep angle on a quirk by Br. Donald, who planted both cherries. The slant proved to be stylish.

WALKING PRAYER

I said the Divine Office at the hermitage while strolling through the grass with my feet bare. Sometime after Lauds I took up with dance or was taken up with it. In that rather isolated sward and wood, the time, space, and privacy allowed for such freedom. Short grass in the big yard remained covered with dew as the sun grew stronger. With feet contacting and feeling ground, I explored the world for what it presented at the moment. Each step, each movement, a bend, a turn, a leap disclosed something delightful to my eyes—colored points of light in the grass, prisms of dew changing hue as I swayed. With legs stretched, back lowered, bending, finding sights at every stride. Blue flowers crouched below grass level, their blue intensified by blue sky; yet lower still, an underlayer of miniature three-leaf green in the thousands, smaller than the clovers you know. The sky is a color too pure to be believed, and trees contrast with bold green against blue. A body must simply stretch to this, must bow to know this realm of honor. My flesh took on the freshness of air and light, and sadness washed out of muscles and bones.

I gathered this moment into a poem:

> Arriving sun stretched
> through pillars of trees
> carpets of color
> before my feet.
>
> Day, in this hidden hall of fame,
> is celebrating day,
> with my company alone
> present to honor being.
>
> In honor of being I dance
> while robin concurs
> with steady, steady chirps—
> famous, persistent chirps.

LECTIO DIVINA

Reading during this annual week here is usually long and deep, copious enough to set me on course for the following months. That enables me later to survive better with the shorter spans of reading at the monastery. Hermitage time also allows for serious effort at memorization, and a few years ago I got two or three long poems by Rilke under my belt. It is not enough to get poetry inside your skull. It has physicality and sound that require putting it under your belt, ingesting and getting it inside your body. It takes a lot of work, and I remembered those poems for a year or so. Eventually, left unvisited, unused, they evaporated—gone where? However, if I put my mind to tugging and coaxing one, back it comes, ready to stay awhile for having once been at home in me.

Usually I memorize a poem one line or two at a time. The best hour at the monastery is in the morning, getting ready for Lauds. I read a line, go shave, return to the page, tend to some other detail, return to the page, then repeat the words as I walk to Lauds. Perhaps after the services I revisit the memory. Within a week or so I complete the work, but this is merely the mental part. The next stage is to recite it aloud. That doesn't come so easily, and harder yet is to recite something in the presence of another person. That almost seems like having to start over again. But once I can recite it to someone else, I have truly mastered the poem. I often used poor Fr. Matthew Kelty as my audience, and with all patience, he bore with hearing me stumble along.

Another essential component in my yearly week of solitude is reading Merton's private journals. This makes for good company, and eases into a mutual, shared, living solitude—not only because he lived here, but more because his writings sound the depths of what it is to be alone, reflective, and left to the unseen presence of God who does not need to be seen. To sit is enough, to read and watch early autumn leaf-fall swept down from the maples, to feel the fragrant air, to hear faint bells marking time in the distance.

Merton captured such moments and put them on paper. I need to capture them too, but not to commit them to a page. Yet, thanks to reading Merton, I can better see what they are for all their worth.

The Place Is Your Meditation

Meditation, strange to say, seems less a need at the hermitage. Some days I forget it completely since the whole environment seems a meditation. Quiet activity and changing hours easily slide into meditation and ease off again to an awareness of this place itself. The place is alive. A gray lizard crawls with short stops along the sunlit edge of the porch. His serious, angular head bears notions impenetrable, ancestral memories of dinosaur days. My presence represents a novelty to his long, lonely days, and he shows no doubt I am a mere transient. This porch belongs to him. A mud-dauber wasp buzzes in the window where the channel of the frame forms a perfect canal for her mud tunnel. It proved futile to knock that out, since she rebuilt it the next day. Living with such wee creatures invites the mind to enjoy an intimate sense of belonging. You have to set your mind to this intimacy with other wild and living things. You can also get the creeps about it. Wildlife reminds me there are vital differences and distances where I do not belong, as when the red-tailed hawk "schrees," asserting territory.

Writing either comes spontaneously or not at all. It seems enough to keep a short, daily chronicle, if nothing more, unless a poem comes along begging to be written. A good number of monks and writers who stay here get passionate and find this cottage irresistible for writing and have turned out whole books on the experience—John Howard Griffin; Fr. John Dear; and Fr. Basil Pennington, O.C.S.O.; to name three.

Urge to Dance

I am often inclined while here to express inspiration in dance. Later this week, the sky moved my feet. Looking up, I discovered the half-moon dancing in a circle, forgetting I was stepping and swaying in a circle myself. A jet tracer struck a straight line through tree curves and clouds; cirrus horsetails stretched layer below layer to the horizon. As above, so below do I—toss my white shirt, stretch it as a cloud—lifting and pulling, tossing and dropping, working hands, stretching arms. My body draws down to earth, drifts up to sky, each movement unplanned, a surprising, flowing symphony of what the heart wants to do next, then next, then next. At last the shirt is tossed high, a wannabe cloud, caught and tossed, released to a life of its own in the breeze, the flight, the falling and catching.

I came to the hermitage in need of cutting free again, as I often once did, starting in 1973 when I attended a workshop in symbolism. One of the practices was called "motion to music." Dancing was not the point, or watching anyone dance. It was to let the motion be what it would be in you. I continued this practice through many years—great for exercise, great for morale. As things developed, I eventually took to it with a twenty-pound weight in each hand.

These days, all too rarely am I caught up in this kind of misbehavior, and usually only at the hermitage. Last year, I really pushed my limits by dancing to a long scherzo by Anton Bruckner. I always carry him in to help my retreat.

Surprise Visitor

Invariably at the hermitage there will be an unexpected surprise, and this year it was the appearance down the road of a tall man who stopped at a distance once he noticed me sitting there. I waved and beckoned him forward. My philosophy is to let the Lord teach me by interruptions. In this case it was not so strange at all—no stranger he was, but the friendly and familiar Bill Chapman, a Quaker I met a year ago. He is review editor of *Friends Journal*, a leader, teacher, and organizer. He is very concerned that young people are not joining the Society of Friends, and that America has only one hundred thousand Quakers today. He was a friend of

Dan Berrigan's since days he spent as his student at Berkeley decades ago. Bill stopped by, and we exchanged some stories about John Dear, our mutual friend, a strong, vocal opponent of war who is in many ways carrying on the late Fr. Berrigan's legacy.

THUNDERSTORM

A retreat is not complete without a good thunderstorm. This broad porch serves as shelter to watch it all develop. Then, the seclusion allows you to go out like a fool and get drenched.

This retreat, no rain came all week long until the last day, late afternoon, and then the downpour was gratifying and robust. Eventually clouds broke and sun came through while rain continued, showering sunlight and rain together. I cartwheeled, became a child again, back in my home yard, knowing only this yard as the whole world, suddenly changed into something wondrous. Rain glistened, back-lit by the sun, showing every falling drop for all its worth. Rain appeared to be falling from the sun itself. This rain was meant for this space, felt like something made for only here and now. The narrow yonder of the field where trees attend Our Lady's statue took on a magical, silver sheen where air misted—a lost wilderness, reverting to some ancient, mythical epoch.

The shower lasted long enough to really cleanse me. The hermitage had been swept and cleaned, and I made ready to depart for Vespers and to return to the monastery totally refreshed.

That evening there happened something of a sign. While laying out bedding as usual on the lumber-shed porch, I saw something I had never seen before, something so unusual I will probably never see it again. The clouds in the east were piled high, lit pink-rose by the setting sun in the west. Suddenly lightning flashed outward in a curious circular array, spreading from a center, coming from no cloud, but from midair in empty space. Soundless, jagged lines stretched out in all directions like a baroque eucharistic monstrance, a wrought-silver sunburst, a complex web of jagged, brilliant netting, briefly seen and gone. All I could do was tell myself that had to be a once-in-a-lifetime apparition. Heaven and earth had kept company with me.

OUR GOLDEN AGE OF HERMITAGES

I was given the caretaker's key to Fr. Louis's hermitage. I never aspired to have that job, but now that I do, it is not incongruous, since I am one of the few who remember its construction. I can still imagine when nothing was there but a broad, appealing clearing on the edge of a forest, a quiet spot to sit on the ground, lean your back on a tree, and open a book. After discovering it, I learned that it was already a chosen spot of Fr. Louis and that he had his sights on that location for the hermitage of his dreams.

And dream it was, for at that time Cistercians, by the order's legislation, were forbidden to live in hermitages. We were exclusively cenobites, living in community, and if you wanted eremitical life you had to transfer to another order. Making such a transfer was another dream of Fr. Louis, but our then-abbot, Dom James Fox, by one strategy or another managed to keep Merton here. Dom James proposed a "third option"—to let Fr. Louis live part time in solitude and continue in community part time. This state of affairs prevailed for five years until the general chapter modified the legislation and Cistercian monks everywhere began to speak up and request a move to a hermitage. Within two or three years, various hideaways cropped up like mushrooms around our woods and fields. With our nearly 2,500 acres, there was plenty of room. And many spots called to many hearts.

There is something about certain locations that begs for a hermitage, long before any hermit comes around looking for a site. Fr. Flavian Burns, while roaming the woods, discovered a perfect fit for his spiritual temperament, a hidden valley of deep seclusion, small and very private. He was my junior master at the time, and I told him how I wandered into this awesome spot. He surprised me by saying he had already decided to build there. The place had struck me as too frightfully secluded for the likes of me. Within a month or two, he and one of our lay brothers began building there. These two solitary locations reflected the respective temperaments of the two aspiring hermits: Fr. Louis's with an open view stretching miles to the distant ridge and Fr. Flavian's surrounded by trees and very closed in, confined, and rather difficult to access.

A HIDEAWAY

Fr. Flavian built a cedarwood structure with a sitting room lined with large, small-pane windows on one side, facing the open end of the wooded valley. The chapel room was small and had an unusual crucifix with a dark corpus made of cork. It leaned down from the shadows above the altar. I have never seen the likes of it—thick, simple, childlike, and somehow comforting. Fr. Flavian lived but a few years there before he was elected abbot, and retired back to it after his resignation five years later. He cultivated and often advocated for us juniors a very simple practice of "pure prayer," wordless and quiet. For the Divine Office at the hermitage, he did not follow our structured Liturgy of the Hours. He read straight through the Psalter from beginning to end in a week. He continued to receive monks for spiritual direction, sharing his mature vision of contemplative life. A group of younger monks also regularly met for discussion on themes such as the philosophy of the person, using a book by Romano Guardini or something by Kierkegaard.

Merton's hermitage, by contrast, was white, with a wide porch open to the breeze. The striking image in his chapel, besides the many icons, was a sunburst with a joyful, serene face in the center. It was painted on the door of the tabernacle, and I suspect Fr. Louis was the painter because of the light touch of the brushstrokes. Above it was Rublev's Trinity, an icon of Mary and Child, one image of Elias the prophet seated by a cave, fed by ravens, another of Elias ascending to heaven in a fiery chariot.

Years later, when these hermitages were unoccupied, other monks were permitted to use them. Some make an annual weeklong retreat there, as I do, or stay a shorter time. All that remains of Fr. Flavian's place, after many occupants and years of use, is a concrete slab. The cedar structure has not been replaced; rather, a new structure was built nearby on higher ground. It is now used part time by another monk.

THAT ORIGINAL GETHSEMANI HERMITAGE

I remember when Fr. Louis's hermitage was constructed in 1960. After the ground was cleared, it was graveled over and prepared for the concrete slab pour. Fr. Louis was with our small group of novices helping out. He was bursting with enthusiasm, and when the roar of a motor sounded in the distance, he hurried partway down the road to see if it was the concrete truck. I made some snide remark about his need for detachment. He responded with a fake laugh, equally snide. With that, I sadly missed a beautiful moment to enter into the joy of a new beginning, and was left feeling in a split.

Later, there came a merrier moment regarding an attachment of another kind. I was preparing to run a telephone cable to the hermitage. At that time, as a junior professed, I worked for our electrician, Br. Kilian. I had learned the skill of climbing a power pole with spikes and belt and could use a pulley to raise a cable. The pulley was called a "come-along," and the cable clamp was called "the attachment." In making preparation for the climb I said, "I have to get my attachment." Fr. Louis lifted his voice: "Br. Paul, I told you that you were not supposed to have attachments."

Installation of a telephone seemed urgent because during the time of Fr. Louis's civil rights writings, a man appeared at the gatehouse with a rifle and asked to see him. That sent out a scare, and some security measure seemed advisable. So a phone was run to our in-house telephone system. Later on, a two-way radio was installed. The only actual emergency I ever heard of was a time when a brushfire started and our neighbor Freddy Hicks was called in to help. When he arrived, Freddy said it looked to him as if Fr. Louis was exhausted and would have killed himself trying to put out that fire alone.

One charmed evening, after Fr. Flavian had settled into his own newly built hermitage, I stepped outside and saw a rainbow in the northeast, one end resting on the woods where Fr. Louis's hermitage was located and the other end resting where Fr. Flavian's was hidden. I could only think that was a celestial sign of their spiritual bond that had now seen its way to completion, a witness to their mutual vision of the hermit life, a gift for the community opening new possibilities.

AND THEN A SHANGRI-LA

Of the three large hermitages at this initial stage, the most remote and difficult of access was the one built for Dom James, who retired there in 1968 after a short stay in a trailer during the time the main hermitage was being constructed. This hermitage location was a thirty-minute drive away, up in the knobs across the valley south of the monastery. To get there required the Bronco, a small jeep of 1960s vintage, with four-wheel drive. Once you crossed the level valley, you took a sharp turn up a rough, steep dirt road that tried the Bronco and the driver's nerves for all they were worth. The ascent was wooded, and the edge of the narrow road dropped severely. Upon arrival, you saw perched in a clearing only what appeared to be a pyramid of stones with a narrow slot of a window. This design was tribute to the primitive cells of the Desert Fathers. The view beyond was vast, the sky open and unobstructed. To enjoy the scene to full advantage, one stepped around the building to the farther side, and there I was surprised to find this was a steel and concrete structure entirely glassed in. Three wings cantilevered out from a concrete base—one wing a porch and entrance, another a lovely chapel, with altar and tabernacle, and the third a living room. The kitchen, bedroom, and bath were centered more privately atop the concrete foundation that supported the beams.

The designer was Br. Clement, the cellarer, who had previously worked in the offices of Frank Lloyd Wright, and the elegant style made that completely evident. He desired to give his retired abbot the best accommodation he could imagine. He often referred to Dom James as "Papa," as did many of the brothers who worked closely with him—a nomenclature I personally could never stomach.

Whenever I visited Dom James in this high seclusion, he seemed changed from his previous character, vastly more cheerful and outgoing than when he bore the burden of office. That job required great responsibility and worry for six other monasteries of our founding, not to mention our own community, which had grown to over three hundred under his care. I withheld judgments and suspended criticisms of this high-end accommodation since I had already treated him to enough of that sort of thing when he was abbot.

Br. Clement asked me to provide the hermitage with telephone service. He had the notion that a direct, private line from the monastery was possible, just like the line running to the cow barn or on the power poles up to Fr. Louis's hermitage. Except this was a seventeen-mile stretch! I was still inexperienced enough to think I could do it. Br. Clement believed that the Campbellsville telephone service was not trustworthy, or perhaps not private enough. I made several calls to the telephone company to obtain permission to use its poles, and had a visit from its kind, soft-spoken manager. After some go-around, Clement settled for a line from Maw Bell to the junction box at the top of the hill, where I would run a line along the ridge to the hermitage. It was all a bit of a game, since the company could have easily run that last jag as well.

So I loaded a cable reel onto the Bronco, drove up to the high chateau, and was greeted with sweet alacrity. I kick-rolled the reel along the narrow ridge into position, and then the inevitable happened. I lost control, and it rolled down the wooded hillside. Dom James immediately laughed, struck with the hilarity of the situation. Then, as I hurried down to retrieve the thing, he got worried, called out, and said we should run for help. Fortunately, the cable reel had lodged against a tree not far below and I was able to roll it back up. I had the cable strung up by the end of the morning. The next day I found the whole story had passed swiftly around the monastery without my having spoken a word about it! Dom James must have made his first call on the new phone to tell of my adventure.

Not long after all that fuss and bother, Br. Guerric came up with another solution to the communication problem: a radio transceiver, with the monastery transceiver in the monastery garage. This idea should have been obvious in the first place. Later on, a third set was placed in Fr. Louis's hermitage as well. When I installed that one, I said, "Now you can call Dom James on the other side of the valley." He did not want to have anything to do with that.

Dom James was very frugal about heating expense. He kept a close check on the electrical meter gauge. One winter day, Br. Guerric, his frequent caretaker, arrived and found him seated in the cold hermitage with blankets wrapped around himself. He would not allow anything beyond his ration on the meter. Likewise, his diet, which was already minimal during his years in community, remained so. As one of the cooks, I prepared him one slice of beef, a bowl of scrambled egg whites, and a glass of milk every day. Beef was an exception to the community vegetarian diet and he needed it because of his bad stomach, ruined by too much fasting when he was young.

This remote Shangri-la afforded a solitude he had long desired, ever since his time as abbot in Georgia in 1946. Little did anyone know, during all those years when Dom James was firmly resisting Fr. Louis's requests to withdraw to a hermit life, that he himself longed for the same.

With all these hermits surrounding our community, I found some sense of spiritual support. While meditating after Vespers, as I slowly paced the walkways of the "preau" (the monastery's inner courtyard), I would remember Dom James high on hills across the valley, knowing he focused on the same Presence as I. He liked to call it "the prayer of simple regard." He and the other hermits nearby seemed to enhance the community prayer through these multiple expressions of our prayer life.

Once Dom James was free of abbatial responsibilities, he could pray as long as he wanted, and his private Mass was interspersed with long periods of silence. Altogether it lasted three hours, as did the Crucifixion. A former monk told me recently that, after he left the monastery, he occasionally returned and attended Dom James's Mass. In the extended intervals between Mass prayers, Dom James seemed to drift off into a mystical silence.

This mountaintop life ended abruptly in 1977, on the Saturday night after Easter, when two local men entered Dom James's hermitage, tied him down, cut the phone wires, and ransacked the place—including the tabernacle, which they must have imagined to be a safe. Shocking to them, they found no money, although there was an envelope of cash for Mass stipends lying on the big table, and they stole

Dom James's shotgun, which he kept nearby for the occasional rattlesnake. The next morning Br. Guerric received no answer back from his regular Sunday morning radio call, so he immediately drove up and found Dom James still wired to the bed. After that, the old man no longer felt secure in the hermitage. That was the end of his days at the Shangri-la. He retired to the monastery infirmary, saying daily Mass in the infirmary chapel. The property was eventually auctioned off and sold to a businessman in Louisville as a hunting lodge. As you might expect, without a regular resident it was soon vandalized and left with smashed windows. I saw a recent photograph with a rattlesnake in the ruins of the chapel.

Neighborhood rumor confirmed what I suspected: the two men were put up to that dirty job by local marijuana growers. With the market expanding, these weed growers moved in during the 1970s and were farming summits of the knobs. Police cars on highways below could not detect marijuana on the wooded elevations. What is now famously called "the Cornbread Mafia" did not want monks driving where they might detect and make report of the plants. Lebanon and Raywick, nearby, were the hub of what became the biggest drug cartel in America. We monks knew very little of it at the time.

Dom James personally knew one of the two intruders because the monastery had recently built him a house. After the man was imprisoned, Dom James took up a letter correspondence with him, and that friendly relationship continued until Dom James died.

BR. ODILO'S WHIMSY

The wind of enthusiasm over eremitical life continued into the 1970s and affected all levels of the community, high and low. Some were naturally loners, others zealous community men who had devoted much work to our life. I cannot resist including a profile of some of these unusual characters.

With no one really noticing, there cropped up a random, thrown-together shanty. Br. Odilo built it tucked away in the woods across a field from Fr. Louis's hermitage. It was composed of scraps and leftovers from many construction projects completed or underway at the monastery. This fantasy hovel reflected Br. Odilo's unique and peculiar, if not feverish, imagination—something he alone could have devised. The construction was as whimsical and unpredictable as his personality. There was no floor plan, only small rooms to fit his small body, and a vertical window wedge jutted out of the roof, perhaps to allow a watch on Fr. Louis on the far side of the open field. Fr. Louis with chagrin noted in his journal that this was an encroachment.

Odilo was short and solid, had a red beard, and was gifted with a marvelous Irish tenor voice. He never learned how to read music, was never a choir monk, and never sang on the schola. But in his later years he spent hours singing along with records of famous opera stars while tape-recording the results. He loved to stand a long time looking out a window gazing at the sky. He seemed a lonely man, and when he walked through the kitchen he would say, "Just passing through." Perhaps that fits as an epigram of his life. He suffered bipolar episodes from time to time, making him wild and hyperactive. He wrote a whole book of intellectual ideas that no one could follow except Br. Victor. Whatever that book was about, it made Victor laugh out loud, even in the scriptorium, where strict silence was to be kept.

Odilo's shanty has fallen into ruins, and remnants can be found in the overgrowth of the forest.

TRAILER HERMITS

For several monks, the actual structure was a matter of indifference; it was the remote location that counted. One quick and easy way to enter upon a hermit life was to convert an already-existing outbuilding. One such was "the pig house," a small farrowing barn that had been abandoned. It was cleaned up and occupied by Fr. Alan. He had once worked there tending pigs, but no one any less dedicated to solitude would ever think of staying in a pig house even one afternoon.

Another quick and easy solution was to acquire a used trailer. Fr. Hilarion lived in one for many long years. It was reached by a drive through a pine forest and was surrounded by trees, affording no view at all. The feeling it gave was one of complete privacy, good for inner focus. For a while Hilarion was my confessor and adviser, back when I was a novice. With him I felt free enough to express some of my more radical ideas. If he disagreed, he countered by pushing my ideas to their logical conclusion. I would agree to the conclusion, and he would say, "Well, at least you are consistent." Hilarion was a strong-willed person and would have left the monastery for the life of a hermit, but some accommodation was made and he stayed, working part time as chemist for our cheese lab. He interrupted his hermit life to serve as novice master for a few years, and eventually returned to the trailer.

Fr. Louis admired Hilarion and said, "He knows what he wants." When he made that remark, I immediately replied, "I know what I want, and I want it now!" Fr. Louis flinched and said nothing more, but the next day he read something out of his private journal about an unnamed young man who came in and expressed how he wants it all now. He did not name me as that person, but it was enough to turn me away from thinking that maturity is about wanting anything and everything now. What you want can only come over a long period of time and takes patience.

The monks moving into trailers had spent many years in the monastery, a precondition laid down by the Rule of St. Benedict. One such veteran occupied a beat-up trailer in a cow pasture under a small oak grove; he was the notable Fr. Chrysogonus, our musician and world-class scholar who had gained a reputation among medievalists at universities in America and Europe. The front end of the trailer had a study desk and a small piano where he pursued his compositions for the Divine Office and Mass. At the back end was a tiny chapel. In the middle was a bath with the tub full of manuscripts and rare books, but not for bathing. Within a year he composed the whole liturgical cycle of music, all rendered in a plainchant style. Since he took certain musical liberties, he claimed that the work was disqualified from being called Gregorian chant. Nevertheless, it was simple, had character and elegance, and endured as a perfectly monastic musical expression. The antiphons written by Chrysogonus for the Divine Office continue in use to this day at the abbey, but the new translation of the Mass Lectionary has required new musical settings. These are being creatively accomplished by Br. Luke, remaining in continuity with Chrysogonus's simple, musical sense of words and following Gregorian modes, without being imitative of "the Maestro" (as we called him).

Fr. Chrysogonus exemplified what came to be known as a "semi-hermit" life. He spent some time at the monastery, chiefly to accompany the choir at the organ or to give conferences. Annually he flew to Europe to rifle libraries for unknown or unexplored manuscripts. He disclaimed being a hermit and said he only needed time and a place to work. I know in fact he had a strong love for solitude. As years passed, he moved to larger accommodations as one or another hermitage was left unoccupied. Each one was soon piled high with books, musty manuscripts, documents, and stale air. He kept windows closed to protect the old volumes from the high humidity of the Kentucky climate. Once he began using a computer, all the curtains were drawn and the room was left dark as a cave except for a small desk lamp. Although each of his hermitages seemed to be a chaos, Fr. Chrysogonus remembered where every single book, note, and scrap of paper was located.

CHEESE BOXES MAKE AN ARK

One of the smallest, most novel, and frugal designs for a hermitage was hand constructed by Br. Rene. He was skilled at raising cows and farming, and was especially devoted to the Rosary. The structure was assembled to be mobile, mounted on long steel skids, and neatly constructed out of discarded cheese-top boards from our wood-planing shed. These planks were ½ inch thick, 6 or 8 feet long, and lined with 6-inch holes. These were carved out and removed for use as tops for our round, wooden cheese boxes, marketed as gift items. The remainder board was discarded. Br. Rene, always concerned about poverty, salvaged hundreds of these boards and layered them horizontally flat against one another so that they stacked up as solid walls. The outer and inner facades were unbroken and the holes were buried within. The building's external surface was then stuccoed against rain and insects. The space inside, measuring about 8 feet by 16 feet, was roofed over with curved corrugated metal. The simple structure was christened "The Ark." Rene hitched it to a tractor and slowly dragged it on its two skids a mile and a half to a lonely place at a forest's edge bordering a field. The Ark was used part of the time by Br. Rene, and others took turns using it as well.

The Ark became a permanent residence for Fr. Roman Ginn, who lived there for over a decade. Fr. Roman had been one of the founders of our monastery in Chili and eventually took up life in the Andes as a hermit, serving as a village pastor. His appearance was as close to a Desert Father as you might find. He was small and thin, had long, stringy gray hair and a long, scraggly beard—and had a twinkle in his eye. The Ark had no electricity or running water; Fr. Roman cooked on a woodstove and raised a garden of butternut squash and other vegetables. On Sundays he walked to the monastery, concelebrated at community Mass, and returned with food in a backpack, carrying water in plastic milk jugs. A certain wealthy visitor from Louisville once decided Roman should have a donkey to ride. So a barn was built near The Ark, and then a second donkey was added. Their names were Hosanna and Halleluiah. Roman fed and watered them daily but never took a ride. He called them "my lap donkeys."

FR. MATTHEW'S FANTASIES

Much-beloved Fr. Matthew Kelty, known for his memoir, *Flute Solo*, and for his published collection of homilies, devised various places of recluse. These might be considered as warm-up practice for his later experiments in North Carolina and then New Guinea, where he lived alone atop an extinct volcano, looking out over the ocean toward several others. Having lived in solitude as a missionary before entering the monastery, he wanted to return as a Trappist to deal more deeply with feelings of loneliness.

In the first of these warm-ups at Gethsemani, soon after finishing his novitiate with Fr. Louis, Fr. Matthew converted an abandoned dynamite shack located on a hillside above a cave. There he installed a potbelly stove, a desk, and a chair. He put a short, white picket fence around it and planted daffodils in the yard—sort of a child's fantasy, rather redemptive of the original purpose of the shack, which held explosives. The dynamite once stored there had been used to blast out the cave, which would serve as a community bomb shelter in case of nuclear attack. These were the Kennedy years, and while Merton was castigating the immorality of such preparations in the *Catholic Worker*, a contrary agenda was at work at the hands of Br. Victor, the cave builder, and Dom James. We had men of all kinds in the community.

A second imaginative, slightly larger refuge for Matthew was the old pump house located below Dom Frederic's lake. Matthew told me I could explore the hut when he was not there. Exploration it was. One approached it by a grassy road through a thinly wooded hollow. It was white and overshadowed by the massive concrete dam behind. On opening the door, I was stopped dead by a blank wall. I could not enter unless I wedged into this tight entry (literally "got myself cornered") and closed the door behind me. Then, everything fell dark. When my eyes adjusted, I could see enough to turn to the left, where immediately I was confronted by myself in a full-length mirror. There were lessons in all this. What happens when you enter solitude? You first get yourself into a scary dark corner. Then you see light, and it is yourself you have to face, approach, and move on from. Next, a turn to the right found me treading the cover of a dark pump well. Would it hold? What subterranean dangers lay below? How secure was the barrier I placed against them? Bravely treading across the grate, I stepped straight into a holy space: seeing an icon of Christ, a shelf with incense, a breviary, and prayer beads. Another turn led to a brighter wall covered with symbolic, enigmatic forms from the I Ching—an ancient divination text Matthew consulted and studied. Throw sticks and the Tao Te Ching were there, along with Carl Jung's commentary on the book of Job. Matthew was exploring the unconscious, and this bright corner was the station of enlightenment. A fourth turn brought me to a happy scene, a window looking out on the woods, on a shallow pond of dark water, and the road I arrived upon. A guitar hung on the wall as did a cowboy hat; there was a rocking chair, a bookcase, a landscape painting—a place to relax and reflect.

Such runs the course of the solitary life as Matthew understood and practiced it.

THE STONE HUT

Our farming fields have many sandstones, and some brothers once gathered and put them to good use. This was for the most laborious construction, and perhaps the most futile, which we called "the stone house." Never was it occupied; it served more as a curiosity than a place to live in. Its most remarkable feature was its four corners, constructed of hexagonal stones that once served as pillars in our church. In the church renovation of 1967, the plastered stone pillars were replaced by steel H beams. Many of the stones from these pillars can be randomly found around the neighborhood, some were given away to workers, and one is even in St. Louis, Missouri, on my brother's front lawn.

Br. Wenceslaus, who worked on the church construction, needed to occupy himself with a new project once the renovation was completed. He was impressively muscular and loved that kind of heavy work. So with the help of Br. Brian and me, the foundation was dug and large fieldstones were laid. One afternoon I was alone laying stones when a car drove up and parked forty yards away. Fr. Louis stepped out with a man and a woman. He lifted his arm, yelled "Hey Paul!" and waved me over. The couple were Jim Holloway and his wife Nancy, who taught at nearby Berea College. Jim was editor of a unique journal, *Katallagete*, which was mainly Southern Baptist in content but with leanings to the left in favor of civil rights and opposition to the war in Vietnam. A cooler of beer was hauled out (these were not your usual Baptists), and we took turns cracking open those snap-top cans. When the first try splashed on me, Nancy said these cans were like Lyndon Johnson's foreign policy—they blow up in your face.

Fr. Louis inquired about the stone hermitage and said, "Who is going to finish it?" I was puzzled by the question, and later discovered what Fr. Louis already knew. Br. "Wincey" was going to leave the monastery. I should have guessed it already from clues that had been dropped. A few days earlier I'd heard Wincey and Br. Coleman, the other construction boss, addressing one another, using not their religious names but their secular ones, Frank and Marty. They both left and went their separate ways.

Somehow the small, solid, one-room construction was completed; however, I lost interest in it. No one ever moved in, and it barely got any use. It is standing evidence to an overflow of energy expended on hermitages. Today it remains on a road where retreatants walk, and the surrounding forest makes the atmosphere close, windless, and stifling. Recently, it was restored by a man from Bardstown, Dick Walsh, who had once been in the monastery. It is now something of a stopping place where retreatants sign the visitor's book, say a prayer, sit awhile, and pass on.

Fr. Augustine's Chicken Gallery

Fr. Augustine was an in-house hermit who began with a tiny room by the bakery with a sign on the door: *House of 10,000 Things.* On entering, I could easily believe that, since everything imaginable could be found there. Fr. Augustine nearly burnt the bakery down by tumbling a stack of paper onto the hot plate. Later he moved to a large abandoned chicken coop that was about 50 feet by 30 feet. It was brightly lit with a high clerestory. He used it as a studio, made carvings, and painted canvases of monastery landscapes or fantasy elves playing on his work desk. I have one in my office, a strange symbolic, theological composition about heaven and hell. Fr. Augustine sculpted, wrote poetry, translated, and even took to knitting in the final years. He had his own book collection on art, photography, and crafts and an extensive library on Oriental religions. He was a renaissance man in his haphazard way.

Fr. Augustine came to the monastery as a widower, had a grandson living, and had been ordained a priest in Brazil. In his youth he had traveled Europe in a family circus as a clown. He lost his leg in a motorcycle accident, and during his monastic years was heavy and clumsy on his feet. He taught languages and theology to the monks, and I learned some Greek thanks to him. He had a keen interest in

Buddhism and Hinduism, and spent hours discussing them with Br. Harold, the infirmarian. When he served as my spiritual director and confessor, I would ask him a question on some point of morality or theology at the end of my confession, and he would eloquently carry on for another twenty or thirty minutes. He had something of a British accent and constructed long sentences beautifully. That alone was an education for my untutored ears.

Before he died, he told Br. Harold of a vision he had in the hospital. He saw the whole world, and one by one he saw cities drop away, then lands and seas, and the people within them dropped away. All time ended, he said, and all that was left was the eternal Christ. "Please go," he said, "and tell this to the brethren."

Hermitages have had their day. Like mushrooms, they emerged and vanished back into the ground. Fr. Augustine's studio was leveled last year, and now nothing is there but a grassy yard. Today, in fact, only two hermitages are left, and they are used only part time. I thought that no one aspires to become a hermit anymore, but to my surprise one of our junior monks, nearing his time for solemn vows, departed for a colony of hermits in Maryland. There will always be some hermits in the Church, but whether any will live at Gethsemani again remains to be seen.

I myself remain a nighttime hermit who sleeps like a yard dog outside all year long. I occupy one end of the lumber shed, mostly sheltered from the wind, atop a wide porch slab and under a roof. It faces on the darkest part of our enclosure area, where stars are most visible, where silence prevails in winter, and where summer brings numerous frog croaks, peeper frog peeps, coyote howls, owl hoots, cricket chirps, whippoorwill and chuck-will's-widow songs, and occasionally some screechy thing I can't identify. Oh, not to forget ordinary cows, horses, mules, and farm dogs. I love it. I have done this for twenty-five years now, with a warm sleeping bag for winter and cool night breezes for summer, all as healthy and comfortable as needs be. I experience a special solitude there, a keener edge where no one is within yelling distance. In dark, gloomy weather, it takes some bravery to walk out to the spot, but that is part of the challenge. For the rest of the time, it is like paradise or, more modestly put, brings a merging with the ups and downs of the world around me, its dull and drab passages as well as its charms. Last night, for instance, I awoke to a moon above the pinnacle of a cedar with fog below, glowing low in the field.

Fr. Louis's hermitage continues to be used by various monks for private retreats. (It is one of those remaining two.) Five or six of us spend a full week alone there once a year. How did this happen? After Fr. Flavian's retirement as abbot in 1973, there came a string of three abbots, none of whom particularly favored hermits or even cared to spend a week alone themselves in a hermitage. Mind you, there was never an overt polemic against hermits, only a lack of encouragement, a tolerance, and a clear teaching and understanding that we are cenobitic monks in community under the Rule of St. Benedict.

The enthusiasm Fr. Louis generated for the hermit life gradually subsided out of quiet neglect. However, some mark remains, both here and in other monasteries. It remains as a valid option, allowing, if nothing more, a few days in solitude for any who choose. This is of great benefit for community life, and relieves some of the routine and busyness that easily crowd the heart. Fr. Louis said that a monk should have a window open on the solitary wilderness, and even if you never quite jump through the window, it is good to have that perspective. It accentuates and balances something of what you already have, living in community.

PRAYER NURTURES POETRY

Prayer, mute as the ground, is a seedbed for poetry. Prayer, while at rest out on the ground, catches plenty of seeds. The kind nursery of nature is congenial to prayer and nurtures poetry. They form a symbiosis, like bees and trees, which thrive on one another despite all their differences.

It is quite cogent how psalms in choir, how prophecy and gospel, how all great poetry, nurtures prayer; equally cogent are prayer and poetry. They can do without one another, and often do, but not as well. Like kissing cousins, you have to keep them apart sometimes or they will get to scrapping, get in each other's way, get to too much kissing.

I try to keep peace in this family by balancing heart, mind, and imagination. This is why, in daily meditation out-doors, I sometimes include a haiku, written for the moment.

This brief and concise form of poetry works well to bring finish to a simple and quiet sitting. I sit without cultivating or developing any particular thoughts. After that, it helps to draw to a close by stating something about the moment I am in. Without some kind of a conclusion, the mind easily drifts off into a fog and remains there. The practice of quieting the thoughts, indeed, leads to lucidity, but can easily end up in just the opposite—a gray funk. So I set myself the task of expressing in words what this precise, clear, open moment of awareness has brought me. This enhances the moment, honors our separation, and serves as transition, and I leave restored to a more reflective use of words.

Haiku has the advantage of not demanding too many words. Seventeen syllables, no more, no less, if you are keeping to the formal code. Good writers need not adhere to that, and often use fewer, but I like the challenge, and the precise form makes me write something other than what I would under my own impulse. In collaborating with such a fixed form, thought brings forward something beyond what is contained in the immediate perception. Three lines are mandated: the first with five syllables, the second with seven, five in the third. Nature is a standard feature of haiku. With any rules beyond that, I lose interest. I simply intend to unite mind and matter and leave it at that.

For instance, as I sat on the lawn chair this morning, large birds, four or five of them, were making a show with squeals and quivers. Quite unusual; I wasn't sure what birds they were, red-tailed hawks probably. Not that they preoccupied my mind that much, but every now and then they resumed calls, reminding me they were still around, changing location. They were about the only birdcalls sounding at the time. Eventually, I saw a connection there and concluded:

> Whole family of hawks
> flap and screech. Smaller, frightened
> fowl cautiously still.

In what I write there is a meeting of mind and matter, in the sense of humanizing something—a bird or animal—seeing the wonder of it in terms of lives of our own.

> Dove dredges up deep
> ancestral songs, songs of old
> from eons ago.

Or something such as this about the evening sun:

> Shaggy headed sage
> retires with fond memories
> hiding his brilliance.

I make two daily meditations, one as soon as I wake up in the night at 2:30, saying the "prayer of the heart" on beads (repeating "Lord Jesus Christ, have mercy on me"). That lasts until 3:00, when I prepare for Vigils at 3:15. The second period is immediately after Lauds and Mass in the morning. An hour there of words spoken and sung sets me up to settle into wordless meditation when the mind need only be present, alert, and still. Thoughts may come and go, but these are better left alone since they prove of deceptive importance and become an inducement to sleep. My intention is to be purely open and receptive, and if the circumstance around me has brought something to my attention, I take that as a gift of the moment, a seed to be received. The smallest, most incidental things can be a gift, such as slimy slugs on the wet pavement, or maybe something vast and undefined as weather changing, when I put a name on the mind of the weather (as if weather had a mind of its own).

> Snow melts in cold rain
> with dreams of Siberia
> and long, sad novels.

This unique chemistry of place and time crystallizes into words, participating in the hidden Presence that shapes all things.

> Crows crazy with their
> work-a-day conversations,
> happy at it.

It may be dramatic or not:

> Vast army of trees
> bending backs before onslaught
> of advancing storm.

The mind takes in things and makes something new out of them. Perhaps the mind itself features in the moment:

> Wind feathers snow on
> black asphalt. Patterns shift while
> mind elsewhere drifts.

One need not strain at a spiritual bent to the poem. It will show through by virtue of being true to the moment. Within every moment present there is a Presence. This Presence does not seek any other voice than the present itself. It need not be explicitly stated; implicit awareness is enough. In writing out the moment poetically, play, not effort and pressure, is called for—just a drifting on the current, a personal gratuity drawn down into the gravity of the moment. To call it a "prayer practice" is artificial.

"I don't know exactly what a prayer is," said Mary Oliver. However, "I do know how to pay attention."

I am inclined to think that the more a thing is a "practice," the less it is a prayer. You cannot do without practice, of course, but the better you get at it the more you forget practice and go beyond.

Generally speaking, it is perilous to write about one's own spiritual experience. It might be good personal therapy, might serve to clarify the mind, be useful for instructing others or inspiration, but seldom does it make for good poetry. Expression by indirection is to better effect. "Tell all the truth but tell it slant," says Emily Dickinson.

The Canticles of St. John of the Cross speak in this way of the heart's quest in faith, using metaphors.

> One dark night,
> Fired with love's urgent longings
> —Ah, the sheer grace!
> I went out unseen,
> My house being now all stilled.

When writing is directly personal, the less there is of it the better. When the Thomas Merton Institute sponsored the Thomas Merton Prize for Poetry of the Sacred, I was on the board for selecting the finalists. I found it heartbreaking, because people wrote so sincerely about their inner experience, but it was almost always bad poetry. Writing is a discipline of its own, and requires some objectivity; meditation is a discipline of its own, and requires a distance from words. You cannot spill out your guts and expect it to be good either for poetry or for the guts. Bringing the two together successfully is a happy accident as much as a discipline in its own right. Another name for happy chance is the grace of the moment. And for this there need be basic openness, an ability to receive as well as to create. For this reason, prayer and poetry are in close alliance—in competition at worst, in harmony at best. They follow along parallel tracks, but sometimes they strike an accord. These can result in immortal words, such as St. Augustine's "Too late have I loved you, O Beauty ever ancient, ever new, too late have I loved you."

Battle of Wits with a Mockingbird

Last night, sleeping out on the lumber-shed porch (or what might be called OM Shanty, Shanty OM) was difficult.

> Mockingbird woke up
> Started practicing music
> At twelve-ten a.m.

At first, it was kind of enjoyable. I was awakened from a dream.

> Mockingbird played with
> my half-asleep mind. Each call
> speaks some oracle.

I think this is how the Native Americans communicated with the birds. They lived with an unfettered imagination. Birdcalls were heard as messages.

> He really gets off
> on bright moonlight—goes at it
> two, three, four hours.

He says words like "Raymond"; "Scooby-doo" is his favorite. Maybe that is his name. Maybe birds are always piping out their names, or are calling upon their name for God. And we vulgarize it by giving them names of our own.

This is the third night "what's his name" has awakened me. It is utterly useless to yell at him. He takes yelling as enthusiastic cheers from an audience. So, instead, I used a bit of bird psychology. I took a blanket and flapped it at the cedar. That frightened him into thinking maybe of a large dangerous bird, and off he flew, not far, but enough to allow me to sleep through his sound.

When I rose at 2:30 for Vigils, he was still going on and on, and who knows how long after my departure?

> Pure love of music!
> Audience all gone asleep—
> that doesn't stop him.

There might be a lesson in this for monks:

> In the Latter Days
> when other souls have died off,
> Monks still singing psalms.

Birds live with the inveterate urge to be birds. Monks live with the love of being monks. That is sufficient unto itself.

But I still have to sleep. Next night that showman was back. When he started in late, I was too sleepy to get up and flap a blanket, so I put a pillow over my ear. It muffled the sound and sleep came. But I woke half an hour after my usual rising time. I couldn't hear my alarm clock. Or, subconsciously, I assumed the clock was the bird, since he can sing just like my alarm clock. I was already late for breakfast duty.

So I tried a new strategy next—something that works with animals. I "marked" my territory, right under the tree where he could smell it. That night I didn't hear a sound. Peace at last.

Or so I thought. Next night he was back. The "marked" tree was not enough, and the big sheet flap became necessary again.

> I wish talent star
> with night variety shows
> would go off the air.

This little guy is pretty smart. Next night I tried the "flap" again, and he flapped back. I thought he was gone, but in five minutes he was at it, singing strong and clear. He can't be fooled anymore. Just flaps back at me. Later, when my ears under the pillow detected the alarm, I sat up and the bird was answering my alarm to perfect rhythm and pitch. Now he is able to rouse me at any hour he pleases.

> Mockingbird Café—
> All night, newfangled pop songs,
> mostly fandangos.

I can pick out his "take" on blue jay calls—all four kinds—his take on cardinals, including all variations, wrens, and he even mimics other creatures: the peeper frog, tree frog, toad, cricket, and the *schree* of a red hawk.

A good Appalachian girl suggested I use a decoy, some mock image of owl or snake. Okay, I said; an old owl dummy found in the plumbing shop should do. I stood it under the tree out in plain sight. No good. It certainly works for cardinals, and helps clear the cornfields, but this bird is too smart. So I tried propping the owl up inside the cedar tree, left that wicked murderer lurking there. Didn't faze my jolly friend a bit. I had to put my ear under a pillow again. Once more I missed the alarm and arrived late at Vigils, past the first nocturn.

Things had definitely gotten serious! Someone suggested a shotgun, but I don't have the heart for that. Nor heart for cutting down the tree. Then, during Compline came a stroke of genius: I will have a bucket of water ready to splash up into the tree as he sings his lullabies. It worked!

Two nights passed, and when my alarm went off I heard an answer from a distant tree, again in perfect rhythm and pitch.

> Promptly, Mockingbird
> answered my alarm-clock's beep—
> bird to bird heart talk.

So now that the little pagan has been duly baptized, how long will this neophyte Christian remain civil and tame?

Not long. The Fourth of July came, and the sound of distant fireworks got his adrenalin up. Farms all around the countryside throw their own celebrations, which keep me awake. Another bucket of water shut Scooby-doo up for about twenty minutes and no more. Tomorrow I must throw a bigger splash.

I did. It didn't work.

> Sharp and emphatic,
> He celebrates July fourth
> with rousing nonsense.

What can I say? Perhaps he means well—lives a life of service of some kind to his neighbors.

> All night sweet Mocker
> sings lullabies to sad birds
> —everbubby's Mum.

Sorry, child—not!

> The Mocker, all night
> harasses the neighborhood
> —damn sociopath!

So, Independence Day or not, I gave up in defeat, dragged my mattress off the porch onto the gravel fifty feet away. The galaxy above me leaned luminous to the horizon.

I gladly lay awake—almost like watching the face of God. "The crowded stars seemed bent upon being understood," G. K. Chesterton once said. Plus, something was special about this particular night. The space probe Juno was scheduled to arrive at Jupiter and go into orbit, a very difficult procedure. That was worth holding in mind as I watched the night. Thank you, Scooby, for the historical night watch.

All of this nightly go-around with an innocent mockingbird is surely measure of the deterioration of my spiritual life. Two years ago I had a cordial relationship with another mockingbird, a real gentleman. It began by a calm, neighborly conversation after I lay down. As he perched above, he looked down over the roof edge, turning his head at me with keen curiosity. I talked quietly and courteously to him. He seemed to take well to my tone and meaning and recognized a civil companion. I told him I would be sleeping here, and while I appreciated his talent, I needed to sleep, so asked if he would please not sing a whole lot.

Somehow that worked. If I was awakened by his aria, I said, Yes, you sound beautiful and do quite well. And he sang back. I would say something else and he would answer, and after a while the conversation ended and he was quiet. But, of course, his was always the last word.

That went on through the whole summer. When I awoke and got up, he greeted me, I answered, and the silence resumed. After I folded up the bedding, dressed, and walked away, I would say goodbye, and he would make a brief farewell.

I believe there is a natural sense of courtesy to which animals respond, but perhaps my courtesy is not always so sincere. That kindly bird felt safe having this big-hearted night guard lying nearby to keep predators at bay.

However, this Scooby-doo was not one to let himself be fooled. A mere splash of water was not much of a predator to him. He resumed his nightly repertoire in the evergreen stage. And once more, the battle was on!

Verbose sermon,
from tall pulpit, Mockingbird
just goes on and on.

For my next ruse, I found a rope and tied it around a tree branch. I planned to yank the rope and shake the tree. For two nights he did not appear. I suspected he believed that rope was a snake and so kept his distance. But the snake never squirmed, and he decided it was one dead snake. So the opera resumed.

Mockingbird expounds
encyclopedias, vast
histories of bird lore.

Exempting myself from this education, I removed to a distance, out from under the porch roof where dew condensed on the bedclothes. I slept there well enough. Finally, rising to leave at 3:00, I walked to the tree, fumbled for the rope, and then gave it one big yank with all my weight. He departed in a flash. I haven't heard from him since. I only hear the usual buzz of katydids, frogs, and a Kettering owl across the meadow.

A week later, I detected Scooby's new location—along the front road perched above the parking lot:

His career advanced
to Central Avenue, up
on Sweetgums' Showcase.

I am now peacefully back under the porch roof of the OM Shanty, and I hope it stays this way. But I kinda miss that clever little show-off.

EMILY DICKINSON, SOUL SISTER

Someone I readily speak of as my soul sister, "from the further side," is Emily Dickinson. At times she seems to linger near me. I read two or three of her poems every day and often commit one of her irresistible gems to memory, or polish up one I already know. This may be a form of poetic greed. Like walking into a store, I see something and have to have it. Memorization is a way of building up an inner reserve of received wisdom, a library handy without the smartphone. It has become a part of my morning practice of lectio divina, the prayerful reading of scripture. Dickinson's beautiful texts provide a fine supplement to scripture.

POET OF SOLITUDE

Dickinson probes the depths of experience with imagination, genius, and wit. It is strange how often she thinks and sounds like a monk. Most of her life, in fact, was lived like a recluse. After quitting Amherst College, she lived a sequestered life in her family home. She increasingly kept more strictly to house and garden over the years, and did not even cross the yard to visit her brother. She would not come downstairs and appear for visitors, however familiar they were. This narrowing of living space seemed to expand the circumference of her mind and heart. Her range of topics is astonishing, embracing nature without and mind within,

90

existence temporal and eternal, freedom and predestination, and love both erotic and divine. For me, she shows how a monk should live and develop—open, universal, and all-embracing.

Her prescription for inner growth is a perfect primer for a Trappist-Cistercian novice. "Growth of Man — like Growth of Nature . . . / Must achieve — Itself — / Through the solitary prowess / Of a silent life." This could easily have come out of the mouth of Dom James Fox, my first abbot, who so often preached about silence and perseverance.

What especially attracts me to her writing is how eminently she figures as a poet of solitude. The writings of Fr. Louis have given me a taste for this, and I have often explored how voices outside the monastic tradition have handled solitude. (After Dickinson, Rilke comes in as a close runner-up.) Dickinson covers remarkably well the broad range of experiences from loneliness and isolation to intimacy with Christ. She addresses the inescapable solitude intrinsic to simply being human, a unique person, living in view of the singularity of one's eventual death. She offers caution against the real hazards of living alone while illustrating its higher promise. In her solitude, she discovered contentment in God and repeatedly confessed herself as a bride of Christ. As much as her family situation allowed, she lived in "silence, solitude and seclusion"—to borrow another key phrase of Dom James. Her strict practice of "enclosure" actually surpassed that of most monastics of our day: "I live with Him — I see His face — / I go no more away / For Visitor or Sundown." I myself cannot resist running out to see a sundown, and I'm a monastic scandal for frequent visitors.

EPISCOPAL BEGINNING OF OUR AFFAIR

Time was, when I first began reading her, I just could not make sense out of much she wrote. The words, like foreign strangers, all passed me by—a peculiar vocabulary strung together with disconnected meanings. My mind simply could not take it in. I was well acquainted with T. S. Eliot, W. H. Auden, and a dozen other poets. But Emily Dickinson defeated me. Then in 2004 we had a weeklong community retreat with Bishop Robert Morneau of Green Bay, Wisconsin. He was an unusual kind of bishop, one who liked poetry and confessed to having a special affinity for Dickinson. He also, like me, loved hiking. Now this was my kind of bishop, and we headed out one day to climb the knobs! Daily during the retreat he quoted either Jessica Powers or Emily Dickinson and extracted some rare profundity.

So I made a personal resolution to set my mind to a deliberate effort. Every day I made a pass at it. Many poems were easy, of course, but if I got stumped on one, I stayed with it and did not move on until clarity came. How easily you get tangled up in such lines as "Experience is the Angled Road / Preferred against the Mind / By — Paradox." In the end, this poem proved a favorite of mine. It achieves a succinct, profound commentary on freedom and predestination. Often, my daily Dickinson perplexity required a twenty-four-hour fermentation before I understood anything. I would return to one of her puzzles and then, as if by some global rotation over my cranium, every word suddenly fell into place. Part of her technique is not to tell you what the topic is, so you must start with an untitled riddle and get the fun of working out the topic. Editors later added all the titles in the published editions.

Followed by Fame

Publication, of course, was the least of her concerns, once she had been advised by Thomas Wentworth Higginson to not even try. He found her style "too spastic" and likely to be misunderstood. She continued to write furiously in any case, although subsequently she told her housekeeper, upon her death, to burn all her work. Now that is what I call monastic detachment of the highest order! It is something on the level of St. Teresa of Avila or St. Thérèse of Lisieux, who only reluctantly wrote their widely influential autobiographies under command of their superiors.

Merton, of course, fell far short of this lofty idealism (and now I am not far behind in this lack in humility, given what you're reading now). For a few years, I was the one operating the mimeograph machine and could see how Fr. Louis liked getting things into print, even if it was merely a mimeograph. One day he handed me an essay, newly typed up, and slapped his hand against his hip and blew on it, like dropping a hot potato: the newest writing, fresh out of the oven. I believe writing was in his nature. He was born to it. I cannot claim the same for myself. I write for enhancement of my monastic life. In the last summer of his life, Fr. Louis admitted to those attending a Sunday afternoon conference that writing helped his monastic life. While writing was often a burden and complication, creating conflict in his life, it was a positive part of his vocation nevertheless.

Emily Dickinson is certainly deserving of all the recognition she has acquired—her stature with critics is higher now than ever—but in her own mind she was highly disdainful of publication: "Publication — is the Auction / Of the Mind of Man / . . . reduce no Human Spirit / To Disgrace of Price."

So why do I seek to have my mind published, and not follow her fine example? I can't blame it all on the influence of Fr. Louis—I cannot compare with his irresistible talent. And I have less of an excuse. I might offer that I am swayed by the tide of his charisma, and take that fortunate circumstance as the course of the life I have been given. The fact is, I did not write much poetry until after many years in the monastery— until, in fact, after Fr. Louis died. Perhaps I felt too overshadowed to dare to try. I lived for decades without writing much, let alone publishing, so writing is not really essential to my nature or to my vocation. I learned to live a long time without it. The dozen or so small books I have subsequently produced are an overflow of my contemplation, a simple way of conveying to others whatever experiences come on their own in my life.

In general, I think monks and nuns should be putting out some token of their existence (however modest that may be) for others to hear. To the surprise of many, this world continues to be a place where monasticism exists, and we monks do well to let people get some whiff of it, whether they take it seriously or not. For my part, it usually surprises me when anyone finds value in what I write.

As for Miss Dickinson, I would sternly tell her that American literature would not be what it is without her. Hers was a work of the spirit, and part of the larger order of things; publication of her extraordinary work had to happen. I cannot resist making comparisons with the obscure and short-lived saints, the young, hidden monastic saints the Church widely celebrates today—I've already mentioned Thérèse of Lisieux, but also there's St. Rafael Arnáiz Barón and Bl. Gabriella Sagheddu. Although unknown to their times, something of their intrinsic worth squeezed its way through the stones of the enclosure wall into the living light of truth. Although Emily Dickinson was no saint in the usual sense of the word, she had a remarkable spiritual genius and an acute consciousness that might have left her with some inkling of her significance in history. Later, in a moment of reconsideration, she acknowledged that fame, for all its dangers, would catch up with her.

> To earn it by disdaining it
> Is Fame's consummate Fee —
> He loves what spurns him —
> Look behind — He is pursuing thee.

LIVING THE HIDDEN LIFE

The only evidence of Dickinson's acquaintance with monasticism was an anti-Catholic polemical novel, *The Romance of Abelard and Heloise*, by O. W. Wight, which her biographers tell us she read. In it, the Cistercian abbot St. Bernard is the villain. A more probable source is *The Imitation of Christ*, by Thomas à Kempis, written six hundred years ago for novices in a monastery, which she also read. The life of a spinster in her era (mid-nineteenth-century New England) was normal and accepted, yet she had something more—an appreciation for and commitment to the hidden life that won her the title "the Myth of Amherst." From my perspective, this again looks like the description Dom James often used of a true monk: "unknown, unheralded, and unsung."

On the day of my arrival at the monastery, I walked through a door with the inscription "God Alone" carved in stone above. The idea was both appealing and appalling to me, for it struck me as too absolute. The motif of the soul as the bride of Christ has never been very attractive, either. Dickinson expresses such notions persuasively, as strongly as found in the Cistercian fathers. She always wore a white dress for its symbolic value, suggesting the novice's habit or a wedding dress:

> A solemn thing — it was — I said
> A woman — white — to be
> And wear — if God should count me fit —
> Her blameless mystery.

Solitude, she sanely understood, can be positive or negative in its effects. "The Maker of the soul," as she once called it, can be dangerous, for it might also seal off the soul in a cavern of isolation. Such seclusion is not for everybody but might be necessary for certain kinds: "The Soul's Superior instants / Occur to Her — alone — / When friend — and Earth's occasion / Have infinite withdrawn." I have known several monks who have this kind of compelling need to remain alone. Paradoxically, the effect for them is opposite to what it might be presumed. As St. Bernard said, "I am never less alone than when alone."

I love being in solitude, but I don't have to be a hermit. I get more than my fair share of solitude by sleeping out on the porch. Use of private rooms within the monastery has become standard in our order. Yet I find some edge of solitude that comes in waking up in the night when there is absolutely no one nearby. If I attempted a full-time solitude I would grow restless, and my sociable temperament would protest. For shorter periods I am fine. Though limited, this modicum of solitude over many years does add up to a significant amount, and I have been fortunate to have these stretches of seclusion. I must credit Fr. Flavian Burns, my second abbot, with the policy shift that allowed all the brothers in the community more periods of time alone. After my solemn profession was a fallow period when I was left to lay more of a groundwork for solitude. It counts for much in life as a refuge and a place to find strength when life gets complicated and busy. It is a matter not of seeking special spiritual experiences, but of dwelling quietly on the horizon of the absolute.

It is really something to wake up in the middle of the night and open one's eyes on the long banner of the galaxy, on that sheer abundance and distance. I wish more people could do this. It puts everything into perspective.

A MYSTIC

I believe Emily Dickinson never used the word "mystic," but I am intrigued with the question of whether the designation fits her. By "mystic," I mean someone who directly encounters God, one who enters into close union with the divine where the sense of self as a separate entity drops away. There are times when she evokes the direct encounter with God in words so uniquely her own, with such vivid images, having nothing of imitation, nothing of standard formulations found in spiritual books, that I deem it has to be authentic: "He fumbles at your Soul / As Players at the Keys / Before they drop full Music on / He stuns you by degrees." These are words leading slowly toward a direct encounter. That same poem continues with this: "[He] Deals — One — imperial — Thunderbolt / That scalps your naked Soul." You would have to reach for the book of Job, Isaiah, or Jeremiah to find such raw, forthright expressions.

When it comes to the question of her loss of the sense of the self, the answers vary. Most of what she says sustains a sense of continuity in awareness of individuality, at least in the face of death.

> This Consciousness that is aware
> Of Neighbors and the Sun
> Will be the one aware of Death
> And that itself alone
>
> Is traversing the interval
> Experience between . . .
>
> Adventure most unto itself
> The Soul condemned to be —
> attended by a single Hound
> Its own identity.

I see some development in her beyond this; there are suggestions that she dropped this individuality, or at least questioned it: "I cling to nowhere till I fall — / The Crash of nothing, yet of all — / How similar appears." I think a Zen Buddhist would smile at these lines. A real mystic would not claim to be one, of course, or care to be designated as such, so I regard it best to leave the question moot.

What is both puzzling and authentic is how she can entertain opposite opinions about time and eternity. She lingers on the boundary between the two, jumps from one side to the other and back again. Now she is immersed in eternity: "As if the Sea should part / And show a further Sea — / And that — a further." Next in the standard *Complete Poems*, she is skeptical of what is beyond, and remains content with things finite:

> Their Height in Heaven comforts not —
> Their Glory — nought to me —
> 'Twas best imperfect — as it was —
> I'm finite — I can't see —
> The House of Supposition.

Her many-faceted voice finds sympathy even from the atheist and secularist, who can identify with her. Academic arguments will forever rage about what her belief really encompassed, about which side of the fence she actually stood on. She was not one to be given over to easy interpretation, at least not for very long. What does she mean by "Narcotics cannot still the Tooth / That nibbles at the soul"? Is it about doubt, or is it about an inner inkling of the eternal that religion reaches out for?

Fr. Louis found in her a kindred spirit, calling her "my own flesh and blood, my own kind of quiet rebel, fighting for truth against catchwords and formalities, fighting for independence of the spirit, maybe mistakenly, what the hell, maybe rightly too . . . like hugging an angel." I cannot imagine her particularly caring for my embrace, but I do sense a bemused sister standing by, quietly watching me explore her thoughts, enigmas, and utterances.

CONTEMPLATION AND THE CAMERA

I have not had a mystical experience using the camera, and yet, however tentative it may sound, there is some connection between the two. Basically this stems from the connection between the physical act of seeing and spiritual contemplation. The root of the word *contemplation* is the Latin *contemplatio,* which includes the meaning of "to view or survey." The Greek word for contemplation is *theoria,* which means "seeing, looking at, gazing upon." A kindred word from Hebrew is *chaza,* which means "gaze," as in "gaze upon Your face." Most of us know of arresting moments when we came upon a sight, a sunset, an artwork, when we had to stop and take it in. That is a form of contemplation, what St. Maximus the Confessor called *theoria phusike*—contemplation of physical or natural things.

As a child in West Virginia, I had many opportunities to stop, look, and wonder. Our house was in a neighborhood crowded between hills with the street running down the middle and houses on slopes to either side. But a short drive up the high end of the valley opened upon a vista of wooded hills, and we often drove back roads seeking out such locations. There, one cannot travel any distance without driving up, down, or around a curve.

As a novice, I wanted to learn something of the wonders of art and painting. I asked Fr. Louis, whose father was a painter, to introduce me to some good art. He gave me a book of paintings by Paul Klee, the Swiss-German artist whose whimsical vein runs through a range of styles—cubist, expressionist, and surrealist.

Before I entered the monastery, I was moved by photographs of Gethsemani in a calendar that came in the mail in response to my application. A few strong images clearly remain with me, such as the sanctuary with a lamp in the very middle, the walled novitiate garden with novices strolling about, and a walnut tree backed by a view of one distant, symmetrical knob—a tent-like hill embossed as destiny in my imagination, a hill I see daily now that I live here.

A HOUSE TRADITION

Photography has been a part of the history of this religious community since the late 1800s. When I arrived here, there was already a fully equipped darkroom, managed through previous years by a series of able monks. Much earlier, in 1910, a particularly remarkable set of photographs was taken by a Louisville man, Theodore Eitel, who often published in a national photo magazine of that period. I brought this monastery collection, held in our archives, to the public in a show at the University of Louisville photo gallery together with other Eitel prints cataloged there—scenes of city parks and country cottages. There is something fascinating about being able, by photography, to see through the eyes of a man from the past, sights from the distant world of light and shadow that filled the same rooms and grounds I occupy today.

The sense of sight is enhanced in the silence of a monastery. The stricter silence we kept in my early days shifted my attention from ears to eyes. I grew quietly aware of the cloister, yards, foliage, and trees; of the slow, changing angles of light, the twilight and oncoming dark, and the endless play of sunlight on buildings, in halls, and on staircases. For years I was arrested at times by views that seemed special, and then I left them behind. These occasions nurtured appreciation of simply being in this world, in this country-side, in this monastery. It was part of the goodness of life as I experienced it every day. I sometimes thought, wouldn't that make a beautiful photograph? But I never had the equipment to capture the scene and never expected to. A camera was hardly standard issue for monks living in poverty, and only one specific brother was assigned to be the photographer.

Then the day came when I strapped on a Rolleiflex camera loaned to me by the community photographer, maybe on a hunch I might be good at it. With camera in hand, I could stop precisely at spots that caught my attention and capture them on film. Some of these images appeared later in a Cistercian regional magazine, *Monastic Exchange.* Something of what I had seen in good art and paintings in our library volumes was showing through in the photographs. The way to make good photographs is to look at good art and photography. Fr. Louis once told me you learn to write poetry by reading good poetry. He could tell the difference right away in a writer; after reading merely a few lines he would say, "This guy does not read poetry."

LEARNING THE SKILL

I did not photograph habitually until my brother Len gave me a 35 mm Minolta just before I left for Nigeria. (I was sent there to help out with teaching at Awhum, Our Lady of Mt. Calvary, a new monastery of thirty-five Ibo monks, and I stayed for two and a half years.) I wanted to share the sights and scenes and memories. I shipped exposed film to Len, who had it processed in Ann Arbor, where he lived, and returned the photographs to me. I began to study carefully why one photograph looked good and another did not. This was the beginning of learning the art through practice.

When I returned to Gethsemani, the abbot allowed me to keep the Minolta, and I began to produce slides of monthly community events to show at year's end. Eventually I was put in charge of the photo lab, and by one of those quirks of providence there was a visitor on retreat who taught me how to develop film and process prints the next day.

The brother I replaced in the photo lab, Matt Scott, was losing his eyesight and had to let it all go, albeit reluctantly. I can understand why. He had been a professional photographer in the air force (and later a writer for Hollywood movies). He lived as an oblate here, made the oblate promise but never took religious vows. So he commonly went by the name of Matt Scott in-house, rather than Br. Matthew. It was he who had had the unenviable responsibility of taking the famous photograph of the first atomic bomb while on the historic flight of the *Enola Gay*. That alone might have been enough to put him in a monastery, but I never asked him about it.

Another one of my formidable predecessors in the photo lab was Br. Ephraim, who had graduated from the Art Institute of Chicago. I remember him emerging from the darkroom with black rings around his eyes, which did not make the job seem attractive. But I was happy to have the job when it came, and I enjoyed the luxury of a fully equipped lab.

The process still seems mysterious to me—sort of like the life of faith, developing the image of Christ within. You work mostly in the dark, by faith, and don't know what is going to appear on the page until the image slowly emerges. With attention, some agitation, and careful timing, the unseen emerges.

FOLLOWING WHERE THE CAMERA LEADS

The first photography show I had was titled "Through a Glass Darkly"—a reference from St. Paul concerning seeing by faith. My pictures often puzzle the other monks. Because of my love for abstraction, they have often looked and asked, "What's that?"

Fr. Timothy, the abbot, made allowances for my initiatives and development, even consenting to my idea of doing a Cistercian calendar for Cistercian Publications. This came up in a discussion with Rozanne Elder, the editor-in-chief, when she was on a visit. The project involved photographing all the monasteries in the American region. That was quite beyond what our life of enclosure normally allowed. But done in combination with other duties, it seemed permissible. One opportunity to photograph away from the monastery was thanks to Fr. Matthew, whose sister in Boston was unable to visit him. Fr. Matthew hated air travel, so I volunteered to drive him to Boston and photographed the monasteries on the way to the Northeast. The second trip, to the western region, was combined with some theology courses at the University of San Francisco. Again, I drove across the country, stopping at monasteries along the way to photograph in black-and-white with a Leica camera.

The final calendar never materialized. Although my negatives were complete, a personnel shortage at the publisher's offices made it impossible to carry through. Nevertheless, I will always be grateful for the opportunity to see all our wonderful monasteries and experience their spirit. It was also the first time I had been across this land, and the change in scenery was like an ongoing symphony. I had no radio in the rental truck I always drove, and themes from Bruckner ran through my mind. I remember, for instance, the highways on the Great Plains—they were so empty and wide, I could prop up the Psalter on the steering wheel and say the Divine Office while driving. However, that is not something everyone should try.

During one particular phase in my development, I concentrated simply on two-dimensional surfaces—a wall or window frame, sandstone foundation stones with a diagonal shadow skipping across, or a sunlit Virginia creeper casting shadows on stucco. Ordinary objects could be shown as special: scaffolding leaning against a wall, paint patch samplers, water stains seeping down a retaining wall—things that did not seem beautiful became so within the frame of a camera.

A particularly remarkable moment came when I was at our abbey in Georgia, the Monastery of the Holy Spirit. I was attending a meeting there when the first Iraq war began; news arrived at breakfast that bombing had begun. While still enveloped in the shock of that, I took solace in the camera and walked around the cemetery walls, old and weather worn. What was astonishing was that all the images I photographed suggested things like flames, oil smoke, sand—even "a line in the sand" in the form of shades of red, black, and ochre—maps, and aerial photos. I called the group of images "Desert Storm" and included them in my first show, held at the First Bank in Lexington, Kentucky.

Another model of art I have followed is the Zen ink sketch. I admire the simplicity and spontaneity found in this Japanese style, which is characteristic of monks even in the West. I was sent to Mepkin Abbey in South Carolina after Hurricane Hugo in 1989 to help clear the fallen trees. Many live oaks were uprooted, and some that stood had been stripped of their leaves and Spanish moss. What remained were simply the bare, graceful forms. I intentionally overexposed the film to burn out the details in the sky. Then, in printing the film, I underexposed to bring out the texture and tone of the branches. The result suggested Indian ink on rice paper. The emptiness of the spaces heightened the tension of the forms, and the interaction of the two seemed to evoke Buddhist philosophy.

Later I revisited this minimalist ink-stroke style by photographing tar streaks on asphalt roads circling the monastery. These resulted in a busier texture, but dynamic in form. I discovered a kind of sfumato technique of shooting ice on a lake surface with cracks that branched out like ghost trees. Those two image types may be found in *The Art of Pausing*, a collection of haiku I coauthored with Judith Valente and Mike Bever, an aficionado of Eastern poetry.

For a while I developed an impressionist style by photographing through hammered glass, the sort of glass found on a shower bath door, except finer in texture. This was another one of those instances where the camera guided me on the way: I did not really see the picture until I looked through the lens. By turning the focus on the glass, I found that the color behind came through all broken up like pointillist brush strokes. These tinted, hammered-glass windows were in the chapter room looking out on the north garden, yielding blurred renditions of trees, flowering shrubs, and monks.

LEARNING TO SEE

Use of a camera trains the mind in how to see. The intrinsic beauty in things that might otherwise go unnoticed becomes evident when seen through a lens. There develops a two-way partnership with the camera: sometimes I tell the camera what to do, and sometimes the camera tells me. Using an eyepiece is much more effective in this regard, as opposed to relying on the screen on the back of a digital camera. It blocks out all other visual information.

Later I developed an expressionist style that was the result of a week at the Santa Fe Photographic Workshop. It was taught by Chris Rainier, a collaborator and archivist for Ansel Adams. There I began to see people in a less literal and more suggestive way, with blurred focus and moving figures. These were eventually employed in my poetry volume *Laughter, My Purgatory*, published by Black Moss Press.

The monastery is too big to run and fetch a camera quickly when the changing light heightens a scene. So I constantly carry a small camera in my habit's big pocket. Unless I shoot right away, the light will change and the picture is lost. For this reason I first began to carry digital cameras, and have since discontinued film and use of darkroom development. The vision in my right eye has deteriorated enough to make that process disagreeable and nearly impossible.

Taking this quick and spontaneous approach has taught me that you don't really find the picture so much as the picture finds you. You turn around and there it is. Whenever I intentionally set out to "take pictures," I often come back disappointed, with nothing very interesting to show. At other times I might get a hunch, a feeling the time is ripe to go out with a camera, and it usually proves rewarding. This almost comes to me like a call, as if something out there wants to be seen and taken home. I don't know where that intuition comes from. But I now understand that photographing is like a dialogue, collaboration with the world hiding an undiscovered memory waiting to be found and kept. I only need to be attentive, to be shrewd with a click of the finger, with the right angle, and mostly with the right attitude. That is when it all gets really exciting.

CARRYING ON OUR CAMERA TRADITION

The hefty accumulation of abbey pictures that developed over the years was put to good use in a volume published in 2015 by Gethsemani Abbey called *Monks Road: Gethsemani into the Twenty-First Century*. The project was instigated by Abbot Elias Dietz to offer the world a contemporary view of our monastery. It is a modest-sized coffee-table volume with about one hundred photographs, a well-written history of monasticism by Fr. Michael Casey, and a history of Gethsemani by Fr. Clyde Crews, a historian and theologian retired from Bellarmine University in Louisville. No photo credits are listed in the volume, but I took about seventy of them, well selected by Br. Gaetan Blanchette. I did not trust myself to be objective enough about the selection. It was particularly interesting to see how he chose some I would not have, and omitted others I might have chosen. The result was quite satisfying.

In this project, our publishing committee of five was working in a tradition of photo books about Gethsemani that began with *Gethsemani Magnificat* (1949), anonymously written by Thomas Merton, with art editing by P. Wayne Jackson. In 1960, *God Is My Life* was published with photographs by Shirley Burden from New York, an associate of Minor White, Edward Steichen, and Dorothea Lange. Each photo was briefly captioned by Merton in his own handwriting. Another photo book under the copyright of the Abbey of Gethsemani was published in 1966, *Gethsemani: A Life of Praise*. Text, again, was by Thomas Merton and photographs by our house photographers, Br. Ephraim Cole and Br. Pius Pfeiffer. For our 150th anniversary, Dianne Aprile of the *Louisville Courier-Journal* wrote an account of the monastery's history accompanied by a photo collection largely from the archives: *The Abbey of Gethsemani: Place of Peace and Paradox* (1998). Once that book went out of print, we made plans for another photo book. *Monks Road* carried forward a distinguished tradition, this time with images emphasizing the present rather than the historical past.

ASCETICAL CAMERA PRACTICE

If there is such a thing as the contemplative use of a camera, I have far to go yet to achieve it. What it might look like can be found in various models and diverse realms of art. I recognize something of this in Fr. Louis's photographs. For the few years he had use of a camera, he quickly came to contemplation with it in a style of serenity, emptiness, and simplicity. This can be seen especially in *A Hidden Wholeness* (1979) and, recently, *Beholding Paradise: The Photographs of Thomas Merton* (2017), edited by Paul M. Pearson. I was taken by Fr. Louis's winter shots—details of weeds sticking up through the snow, luminous images of the white brick walls in the sunlit corner of a chapel, the wooden slats of a barn side, or leaf shadows slanting across a window with a Gothic peak.

Something of this purity is found in the Cistercian architecture of the twelfth century. The Cistercians manifested an economy of form, a directness that shunned purely ornamental effects but transcended mere functionality. They had authenticity and integrity that bespeaks great respect for the building and materials, and were possessed of a humble sense of the sacredness of the space. Something of this was achieved in the church renovation of Gethsemani completed in 1967. A Jewish poet once put it perfectly in words when he saw the sanctuary: "There is enough room for God!"

In this spirit, I hope, I recently exhibited a series of images of white cowls hanging on pegs. Our halls are lined with pegboards modeled after the Shaker style as seen in Pleasant Hill, Kentucky. The cowls with their long fabric hang in a row when not in use. Morning rays coming through the window highlight the folds and deepen the shadows, and stillness lingers there between ceremonies. When the signal is given, monks come, lift and swing the cowls overhead, and drop them over their bodies.

> Cowls hanging
> on a row of pegs—
> tall disembodied spirits
> holding shadows
> deep in the folds
> waiting for light,
> for light to shift
> waiting for a bell
> for the reach of my hand
> to spread out the slow
> wings, release the
> shadows and envelope my
> prayer-hungry body
> with light.

MERTON'S DEATH AS SEEN FROM THE HOME GROUNDS

My first inkling that Fr. Louis was traveling to Asia was on the day of my solemn vows in June of 1968. As I was sitting on the lawn with my mother and some other family members after the profession Mass, he stopped by and invited me to come out to the lake that afternoon. He said that Bob Lax and some other people would be there. Since I had left the novitiate it had been a hard, long six years, and it was a surprise and delight to have Fr. Louis extend this invitation.

Bob Lax was his poet friend from Columbia University days, and I had read his new book, *Circus of the Sun*. I had long wanted to see for myself whether he fit the description Merton gave of him: "the face of a horse." He did. One of the other visitors was Richard Sisto, a young jazz musician from Chicago who ten years later reconnected with me and became my abiding friend. Yet another was Fr. Vernon Robertson, an Episcopal priest who had recently become Catholic.

"Lax," as Fr. Louis always called him, sat with his gangly legs wrapped around the chair and poked holes in things Fr. Louis said. Fr. Louis glowed with amusement at this old game they played. Sisto's wife, a striking actress, recounted an incident of the previous night when her husband was playing a drum. A moth was flying around a lighted candle, and just as the final slap landed on the drum, the moth flew into the flame. This memorable story became significant for me ten years later.

It happened one morning that I was meditating before a candle when a moth began fluttering around it, and I was reminded of this woman's story. Later that same day, Richard showed up at the monastery, and by chance the guest-master picked me to meet with him for a conversation. We did not recognize each other right away, so it was an auspicious moment when we pieced together when and where we had previously met.

By the lake on the day of my solemn vows, the conversation eventually turned to Buddhism. Fr. Louis spoke of it as a view of life that sees everything as subject to change—*even death*. The addition of that last word suggested to me an understanding of Buddhism that was open to the Resurrection. Fr. Louis complained it was not enough to read what was written about Buddhists by Westerners: "I want to go and gain direct experience and talk with Buddhist masters for myself." This was my first hint about his upcoming trip. I was not surprised when it soon was announced. We had a new abbot that year in Fr. Flavian Burns. Years earlier, Fr. Flavian had told me he thought Fr. Louis ought to be allowed to travel. I was already of that opinion, too, even from my novitiate days. I had a notion he should go to Japan and encounter Zen. "You *ought* to go there," I told him—as if I had some say in the matter. It was just an intuition. It could have been then that I said, "When you die, your spirit will go ranging over the world." He tilted his head back slightly and breathed out, "Yeaaahh."

Through the summer that year, Fr. Louis expressed premonitions that he would die in Asia. He told Fr. Flavian before he left that he might not come home alive. He said something similar to Dan Walsh, his former teacher and friend at Columbia. Dan had retired to Gethsemani and taught those of us who had course requirements or interest in philosophy. Fr. Louis dropped a few other hints indirectly during conferences delivered to the novices and juniors. For example, after a close friend of his died in a house fire, Fr. Louis said a person might have a sense of the arc of his life and of when it is descending to an end. He made other offhand quips such as, "I don't care what you guys do with monastic reform; I'm going to be out there pushing up the daisies."

Occasional comments he made in his private journals indicate suspicions of an early death as well. Briefly, in July of 1965, he referred to "my approaching death." This is in character rather than out of character, since he always lived with the thought that he would die young. In 1960, on his birthday he wrote: "I never thought to have had such a thing as a forty-fifth birthday. Yet here it is. . . . Why was I always convinced I would die young?"

Well, death at fifty-three is young. That's the age at which he would die. But such a thing would be of little concern to him, for he added: "If I don't make it to sixty-five, it matters less. I can relax . . . life is a gift I am glad of."

In September of 1968, three months before his death, while at the Monastery of Christ in the Desert, in New Mexico, Fr. Louis reflected much on death while reading Buddhist and Hindu scripture. Out of the blue he jotted down this ominous statement: "I am not going 'home.' The purpose of this death is to become truly homeless."

I had my own premonitions of his death. A strange image flashed through my mind on the Solemnity of the Assumption that August as I sat outdoors meditating, facing the woods toward the hermitage. I imagined legs disappearing upward into the clouds, the feet wearing work boots such as we all wore. That earthy touch plus the location above the hidden hermitage made me certain the image was about him. Fr. Louis would go into heaven with his work boots on. Just a curious image, that's all, but it kind of scared me.

Eventually, I learned of his forthcoming trip to Asia thanks to Fr. Matthew Kelty, my confessor. Fr. Matthew served as Fr. Louis's confessor as well, and when telling me the news he tilted his head and assumed Fr. Louis's lilting voice: "I'm going to Asia . . . I'm going to see the Dalai Lama . . . he reads my books!"

When the day came for the big departure, Fr. Matthew waited out on the bank beside the highway in hopes of saying goodbye. Like me, he had received his novitiate training with Fr. Louis. These two priests were exactly the same age, born in 1915. I always knew when Matthew was receiving spiritual direction from Fr. Louis because there would be a roar of laughter coming out the window. So for Fr. Matthew, a personal farewell was much in order. Unfortunately, he arrived too late to meet the departing car, and finally he rose to return to the monastery. On the way, he broke out in tears with the sudden realization, "We will never see Fr. Louis again." That Irishman's intuition proved all too true. He was so sure of it that he bid Br. Lavrans, our iconographer, to draw a hand with a diamond in it. That evening Matthew showed the image to the class of juniors lately placed under his direction. He told them, "Fr. Louis is our most precious gift in the monastery and we are going to lose him."

I likewise never found a chance to say goodbye. But a final image of Fr. Louis remains fixed in my mind. I was reading high on the balcony of the library when at a distance he emerged from the exit door of the ground tunnel, turned his back, and walked toward the hermitage. That somehow spoke to me, at that moment, as a definitive vision—his back turned, his head strong with intent, his steady stride away—and I did not like it.

When the official announcement was made of his departure, I hurried on foot up to his vacated hermitage and sat on the floor of the porch, leaning my back against the wall.

Thoughts began to build up to a huge moment. I tried to measure the meaning of this change for him, for the monastery, and for myself. My imagination grew crowded with a picture of Buddhist monks strolling up the lawn in front of me and entering the hermitage. I shied away from such thoughts as too grandiose, but after these many years I see they were not grand enough. The reality has repeated itself over and again, including a visit by His Holiness the Dalai Lama in 1996. But Fr. Louis would not be here to receive any of them—in the body at least.

A few weeks after his departure, a young man came on retreat from New York City. He was a professional dancer, and Fr. Matthew took an interest in him. He persuaded him to dance for the community. There were two performances—one for a select group in the library chapel, and a second one for the community at large in the chapter room. I was in charge of the audio, the recorded music, and he asked for some chant by Tibetan monks. He wanted to dance the journey of Merton to the East. He donned a Cistercian cowl and started at the upper end of the long chapter and danced a slow progress to the exit door at the lower end. When he disappeared, I left the music going, assuming he would dance Merton's return. The chant went on for a long time but he never returned, until I stopped the player and he walked in with the cowl removed. I was a little miffed at why he left out that part.

Another artistic premonition showed up in the parlor where we hang work clothes, the grand parlor. Every monk has a hook and a shoe box in this "boot room," smelly with sweaty work clothes. Someone had placed above Fr. Louis's hook a speckled, rosy painting in the typical psychedelic style of the 1960s. But contrary to what you would expect, it had gothic lettering with the final words for the conclusion of the Mass: *Deo Gratias*. The lettering was rather good, and I thought it would please Fr. Louis to be greeted with such a display of love on his return. But the significance was to be other. This would greet the end of this priest's lifelong Mass, a final tribute: "Thanks Be to God." The sign remained there month after month, far beyond the day of his death and burial.

As weeks passed after his departure, Fr. Louis mailed back brief items of news of the progress of his journey. The monastic conference in Thailand, of course, was to be the climax of the trip. The day came and went while we slept on this side of the world. Of the conference we never heard a thing until the community was seated at its midday meal. Then something unusual happened. After dinner was finished, Fr. Flavian walked to the reader's microphone— something he had never done before. He announced that a message had arrived that Fr. Louis had had an accident and was dead. Details were unclear because telephone service was inadequate. No further information was available, even the exact nature of the accident.

I immediately remembered how Fr. Louis once told our novitiate class that when he died, "I'll need you to say a lot of '*De Profundis's*' for me" (Out of the depths . . .). That is Psalm 130, one of the seven penitential psalms. I left the refectory, walked in a daze to the church, knelt, and said all seven penitential psalms—said them with intensity such as never before, or since. Afterwards, I slowly drifted into the scriptorium, where the fathers and scholastics were quietly at their desks before None. The scriptorium was located above the boiler room, where occasionally, at rare moments, a safety pipe outside the window released steam from the buildup of pressure. As I entered the room, there roared out a white cloud of steam into the air, and immediately came the thought: Jesus exhaled his last breath with a loud cry, bowed his head, and gave up his spirit.

That evening, after Compline, I entered the darkened scriptorium again. Standing at the same spot, I noticed a holy card left on the table. I picked it up and dimly saw, in Fr. Louis's handwriting, "*charitas non deficit*"—love never falls away. It hit me directly—punch to the chest—a message sent straight to my heart from an invisible hand. Those were St. Paul's words, but it was Fr. Louis's message.

After that, time seemed to stand still. And time stayed that way all week. We learned that Fr. Louis died by electrical shock moving a fan with a shorted circuit. I spent a day and a night at Fr. Flavian's hermitage, settling into this new state of affairs. The sense of stasis lingered until the remains arrived from Thailand. It felt much like the days after President Kennedy was assassinated—time stood still. The funeral itself began after a long delay as the casket was inspected at the undertaker's. Time weighed heavily.

The abbot had met with the coroner at the nearby Greenwell's Funeral Home in New Haven, together with Fr. John Eudes Bamberger, Br. Clement, and Mr. P. D. Johnson, a neighbor and friend of Br. Clement. I have learned through P. D.'s son, Fenton Johnson (the novelist and memoirist), that when they began to open the body bag for a viewing, the stench from the body, never embalmed, was so acute that they stopped and sealed it up again. That had to have been a keenly penetrating moment for Fr. Flavian, which is probably why, when I saw him at Mass, his skin was *pink*. With that appalling sensation, together with the fact that he had lost the monk he expected would be the pillar of his future as the new abbot, it is no wonder his skin was a color I have never seen on any face.

For the funeral Mass, the casket rested before the sanctuary step and remained closed. The selection for the entrance chant was an old English hymn, "Now Praise We Great and Famous Men." Fr. Chrysogonus, our organist, asked me, in preparation, to revise the words; so I changed it to "great and worthy men." I did not think Fr. Louis would be keen on being celebrated for his fame, especially at a liturgy.

It is notable that this was the first time a dramatic change was made in the abbey church for the seating arrangement of guests. Both men and women were allowed on the ground floor instead of having to attend from the far rear, up in the tribune. It seemed much in character with Fr. Louis that these changes were set in place for him, especially as he was attended by such eminent publishers, writers, and friends.

At the entrance procession of concelebrants, everyone surrounding me began to sing, and the beginning of the long-awaited moment was finally too much for me. I broke into tears, trying to sing as best I could through it all.

Later, at the Offertory, standing to the far side singing with the schola, I observed how the smooth, gray, sloped coffin nosed against the sanctuary step. It looked like a small gray whale with Jonah inside—Fr. Louis swallowed up and carried back from across the world. And what kind of sign might this prove to be? A sign for now, I asked, and a sign for the future?

After Communion, when everyone was seated, a passage was read from the conclusion of *The Seven Storey Mountain*. It was a brilliant choice for the occasion and, though written early in Fr. Louis's monastic life, seemed a synopsis of its entirety, even down to the present moment. At the end came these words as if spoken by the Lord, words about bringing him to the Cistercian abbey of the poor men who labor in Gethsemani: "That you may become the brother of God and learn to know the Christ of the burnt men."

It sounded like no less than a prediction of the manner of his death—"burnt," but with a burn that was electrical, and now his body was returned to the community of "the burnt men." Recently, I found a foreshadowing of this language in a letter Fr. Louis wrote to Dom Frederic, his first abbot, in preparation for his vows. Fr. Louis gave a summary of his life, much in line with the account of *The Seven Storey Mountain*, ending the letter with these words: "I came to Gethsemani December 10, and was admitted to the community on the Feast of St. Lucy, December 13; and now with many prayers and thanks to Almighty God I beg Him to make me, the least of all His servants, totally His so that my past life of rebellious sins and ingratitude may be burnt away in the fire of His infinite love."

There were various ominous facts circulating within the community. Br. Patrick Hart told me Merton died on the same day of the year that he entered the monastery, December 10, and what is more, that he entered at age twenty-seven and died exactly twenty-seven years later. To clinch the wonder, he died on the birthday of Dom James, his abbot of eighteen years.

After Mass, final prayers were said by the graveside as the coffin rested in light rain. Fr. John Eudes was positioned at the head of the casket. As it was about to be lowered, he put his hand to his lips and touched his hand to the surface. Then the coffin was lowered, and the signal was given for a token number of shovels of dirt to be thrown in. Fr. Raymond, a vigorous man and Merton's monastic senior, was given the shovel. He labored with such gusto that the abbot had to touch his arm to stop him. As he was a writer himself, and of political inclinations that differed from those of Fr. Louis, especially over the Vietnam War, some may have seen that action as reflecting rivalry. I saw it as rough Trappist realism about death and as an expression of years of camaraderie.

When the community departed, I climbed a ladder to retrieve a loudspeaker I had hung in a red cedar, necessary to help amplify Fr. Flavian's soft voice. As I climbed up in the gentle rain and placed my arms around the trunk, the scent of cedarwood sweetened the sadness of the moment.

Ten years later to the day, there was a memorial service with some old Merton friends and neighbors in attendance. This was the first of several commemorations to take place over the following years. Br. Frederic had formed a Thomas Merton group with me and Fr. Michael, which met every month with young men and women from the neighborhood and some nuns. By then, Richard Sisto had returned to the area and moved onto a farm nearby, on a property abutting our own. His friend Fr. Vernon agreed to say a memorial Mass for our group in the guest chapel. Richard played the vibes, I did some singing, and Penny Sisto read Merton's poetry. I had taken a notion to light a flame on the altar as a paschal motif. I found a beautiful ceramic bowl, filled it with lamp oil, fixed it with a wick, and lit it at the Preface. All went well until the Sanctus, for just as Fr. Vernon reached the words "Blessed is he who comes in the name of the Lord," the bowl exploded and shattered. Shards scattered all over the altar and the floor. Only a small flicker remained on the ceramic pedestal. Fr. Vernon, in a perfectly sedate manner, uttered, "Perfect timing!"

The explosion most likely happened because the flame diminished and the sudden cooling of the bowl made it shatter. You could credit that to my ignorance of ceramics—or to Fr. Louis sending up a sign.

UNEXPECTED
VISITORS

At the Abbey of Gethsemani, I find myself walking among saints every day and occasionally among giants, great and holy. The unexpected visitor—why would they come here, of all places—has become almost commonplace over the years since Fr. Louis's death.

Just the other day, I took a strange walk on the wooded shortcut to Fr. Louis's hermitage, enjoying an unusual visit with a most unlikely woman, a folk-rock singer from New Zealand. Her name is Kimbra—lively, graceful, and young, with long dark hair and a yellow shoulder veil draped to the hem of her black dress. I told her that when Joan Baez had visited Merton one day, she could not resist running through the open field. Kimbra is more of a dancer than a runner. Her companion was Lars, a composer from Norway, staid and quiet, a complement to his vivacious partner in the arts. Kimbra discovered Merton in her youth and continues to read him, along with various contemporary and traditional spiritual writers, like Richard Rohr and Jean Pierre de Caussade.

We talked about many things, including a love we share for the essays of Montaigne. I tried to understand what could cause her, a sensitive woman, to be attracted to rock music. Perhaps it is the attraction of opposites. For an introspective type of person, it can be something of a game to play shadows and masks with the outside world. Mae West was an example of such a performer; her apartment was full of religious pictures, and she was very devout. Also recently, a filmmaker who makes "slasher" movies was here on retreat, and we got into a very deep conversation about playing a role while retaining self-knowledge and identity. I suggested to Kimbra this theory about the attraction of opposites, but she did not confirm it; perhaps at least it gave her something to think about.

Another recent, slightly less unlikely visitor I've escorted up this hillside is Pico Iyer, the British travel writer, novelist, and prolific journalist who was then visiting from Japan. (He also graciously wrote the foreword to this book.) Pico is closely associated with the monks of New Camaldoli in California. A journal once assigned him to write about some unusual adventure, so he wrote about visiting their monastery on the coast near Big Sur. He deemed nothing else quite so unusual as that place, their way of life.

We enjoyed a long chat in the hermitage on that first occasion, talking about the tension between a life of solitude and celibacy and the need and human task of coming to understand our sexual lives. Merton was our case in point, since we both knew from his biography that, in the 1960s, he'd fallen in love with a young woman who was serving as his nurse in Louisville. I referenced Emily Dickinson in parallel, quoting from the first and last stanzas of one of her famous poems:

> I cannot live with You —
> It would be Life —
> And Life is over there —
> Behind the Shelf
>
> . . . .
>
> So We must meet apart —
> You there — I — here —
> With just the Door ajar
> That Oceans are — and Prayer —
> And that White Sustenance —
> Despair —

Pico is married and finds the tension between these two lifestyles fascinating. I often find the crisis of romance Merton endured is of more interest to married people than to celibate religious. Perhaps married people have more sympathy and understanding for his love story.

My guestbook of visitors over the years is actually very long, and I cannot resist name-dropping a few of them . . .

SEAMUS HEANEY

The year before he won the Nobel Prize in Literature (1995), Seamus Heaney was invited to Bellarmine University in Louisville to present the annual Guarnaschelli Lecture. The lecture is funded by a leading brain surgeon who had been with me in the novitiate under Fr. Louis. We were the same age, in our late teens, and he left a year after entering. Funny. When he left, I wondered if the boy would amount to anything.

I went to Heaney's talk for Bellarmine students and listened at the back of the class. What impressed me was how he had started publishing poems late in life. He was already old enough to be teaching secondary school when he submitted a poem to a newspaper. It was accepted, and thanks to the encouragement of the editor, he found much confidence, beginning a new phase of life as a writer. I knew how he felt, since I was fifty-four years of age when my own first book of poems was published. I owe much the same kind of gratitude to Marty Gervais of Black Moss Press in Ontario.

The following day, Br. Patrick Hart and I had lunch with Heaney, who arrived here with Bellarmine president Joseph J. McGowan, his wife Maureen, and several others. At the end of the meal, Seamus wrote out a poem on the back of a sheet of Bellarmine stationery. It ever remains my favorite of his—the description of a ghost ship sailing the middle of a monks' choir in ancient Ireland. The anchor gets caught on the altar rail, and the monks are bidden by the abbot to rush to help release it before the sailor drowns in this world's element. The story ends with an amazing switch in perspective as the sailor "climbs back up out of the marvelous as he had known it."

Br. Patrick framed the handwritten poem with a green mat and hung it in his office. He had long served as the abbot's secretary, as well as assisting Fr. Louis. Eventually the frame passed on to me and now hangs in my office, opposite where I am writing. I must confess that I pilfered Heaney's poetic strategy in my poem about the levitation of St. Teresa of Avila and St. John of the Cross. "Nuns of Avila misunderstood / and reported that Teresa and John, / in conversation about things eternal, / had levitated above their chairs." I proposed that was a misperception—the two had remained fixed in the Immovable, while "the chairs, room and world dropped aslant as they are wont to do." From the saints' point of view, the nuns had gone askew. Thank you, Seamus.

I strongly remember the moment of the poet's departure. He said he grew up near Bolton Abbey, a Cistercian monastery in Ireland, and he knew the remarkable abbot Dom Eugene Boylan. He saw his visit here as a renewal of his earlier contact with monasticism. As he left, his sincere gratitude was obvious from the very direct look in his eyes. My polite phrases seemed quite unequal to that moment of intensity.

CZESLAW MILOSZ

Another one of the giants I have walked with was Czeslaw Milosz—a saint perhaps, a literary giant most certainly. When I learned of his Nobel Prize for Poetry in 1980, and later read some of his work, I was stirred with enthusiasm over the thought of how much Fr. Louis would have loved this profound writing. As often happens, I soon found out that Merton did know Milosz, that they had corresponded, and that they had met in person more than once. Their letter exchange was eventually published as *Striving towards Being*.

When I finally read this remarkable correspondence, I was intrigued by the many affinities and occasional discrepancies between the two great minds, especially in their different ways of viewing nature. Milosz charged Fr. Louis with taking a "veiled" look, one too romantic and innocent of the savage and dark elements in nature. Merton saw nature as a consolation, a place of solitude and prayer.

In 1999 the Merton Foundation was looking for a public event to sponsor in Louisville, so I proposed bringing in Milosz. Bellarmine president McGowan agreed to provide the funds, the monastery arranged for the flight, and they left me to make the invitation, with the help of Theresa Sandok (in Polish no less!) of the Thomas Merton Center at Bellarmine.

Fr. Timothy Kelly then granted me the privilege of driving Milosz from the Seelbach Hotel in Louisville to our abbey. He was accompanied by his wife, Carol Thigpen, younger than him by twenty years, gracious, sociable, and attentive to the quality of the Kentucky knobs and ridges as we drove south to the reading at the monastery.

Earlier, from a published photograph, I had recovered a faint memory of having seen Milosz in Fr. Louis's office in the novitiate—a square-faced man with dark, heavy eyebrows. I had passed the open door of the office and later asked who the visitor was. Fr. Louis had tilted his head back slightly, softened his voice, and said, "That was a great man."

I had time in the afternoon, before supper and the reading, to drive the couple to Fr. Louis's hermitage. Milosz hadn't seen the hermitage on his first visit here with Merton. As we stood inside gazing out the front windows, I asked what had happened when he and Fr. Louis met in Berkeley shortly before Merton's flight to Asia. Had they come to terms with their disagreement about nature? I had an impression that the issue mattered much to Milosz and would not allow myself to miss the opportunity to ask him about it.

He told me there had been no opportunity for discussion. They had met at a party where conversation was obstructed by the many friends who had come back from deep-sea diving exclaiming how wonderful it was below the water's surface. Then he added, in his gravelly voice, "As far as I am concerned there is nothing down there but a bunch of monsters." I said, "You mean as with *natura devorans et devorata* (nature devouring and being devoured)?" "Yes," he said. Then, giving me a sidelong look, he added, "That is Manichean, isn't it?" I said, "Yes." He responded, "That's a heresy, isn't it?" I smiled. He as much as admitted being a Manichean by holding such dark views.

After Milosz gave the reading in the chapter room with his ponderous voice, the abbot invited us to the front office for a sampling of Trappist cheese, our fruitcake, and a taste of celebrated Kentucky bourbon. Milosz talked with enthusiasm about a recent visit to the Vatican, where he had done a reading for Pope John Paul II. He had also visited Poland and said the bishops there did not like John Paul because he was too liberal. Then it surprised me to hear the great poet advocate for a new catechism. What would a sophisticated man like him want with a catechism? I wonder what he might have thought of the one that came out of the Vatican not long after that.

I brought up an item from his reading in chapter, a poem in which he described a serene childhood memory, an idyllic setting on a boat in the middle of a lake at sunset. It was hardly Manichean, so I had to ask, "What about that one poem about nature—so beautiful?" He retorted, "I'm not consistent," paused a moment, and then added, "Merton wasn't consistent either."

Nearly the last thing he said before we left the abbot's office was, "I think there can be no creation without sacrifice." That has remained for me as a kind of Christian koan—an enigma, not to be explained too precisely since that would be to profane it. It aptly synthesized what at once is most Christian and most Manichean about the man Milosz. And I cannot help but be reminded of the book of Revelation: "From the foundation of the world . . . the Lamb that was slaughtered" (Rv 13:8).

I remained ever curious about what might have been the eventual influence Merton had on Milosz. A friend of mine, Mike Bever, had a conversation with Milosz once in Santa Clara, California, and asked him what he thought of Merton. Mike tells me that the poet paused, drew a breath, and let out a sigh before responding, "Ah, Merton." That was all. What that meant—who knows?

Be that as it may, his final book of poems, *Second Space*, speaks explicitly about death, the afterlife, and his own experience and argument with God. A long, amazing poem, "Treatise on Theology," bears the stamp of his nuanced thoughts on such matters. The book also includes a long discourse on his distant cousin Oscar Milosz, a poet in his own right and a prominent member of the Freemasons, then so attractive to many European intellectuals. I could see that these were deeply personal poems of Czeslaw's, and how they ran deep.

SR. HELEN PREJEAN

The first time I met Helen Prejean she impressed me as warm, down to earth, and exuberant. She was here on retreat—one of the many retreats she's made at Gethsemani, often during Lent or Holy Week. I had read about her in a review by Garry Wills of her bestseller, *Dead Man Walking*. I had not read the book or seen the movie yet, but I hardly expected her to reach out to me so graciously, so ready to make friends. Her humanity and humor reminded me that such are the people who change the world.

Today, Sr. Helen's efforts to abolish the death penalty have gained momentum to a point where Catholics are a majority for its abolition. Her intervention with the Vatican has brought a modification in the Catholic catechism concerning the death penalty. At the root of all this is a woman who fully loves and embraces the people God brings into her life.

Sr. Helen was the first person to agree to be a part of the Thomas Merton Retreat at Gethsemani in 2000. That event was sponsored by the Merton Foundation and focused on selected individuals in politics and public life. These included a former senator from South Africa, another from British Columbia, the first Catholic priest to be chaplain to the US Congress, and about twenty others. The first evening, over wine and cheese at a reception on the patio of the guest-house, Sr. Helen approached me confidentially and in her deep tones told of a custom for the dead in her home city of New Orleans. Friends and family go with candles to a grave site and pour wine on the grave. "Let's visit Thomas Merton's grave," she said. Soon, a willing group took the short walk, and we circled the grave with wineglasses in hand. While we stood there, Fr. John Dear, the peace activist, gave an account of the retreat in the fall of 1964 at the hermitage, organized by the Fellowship of Reconciliation; it was the beginning of Quaker-Catholic collaboration and included Daniel Berrigan, S.J.; Phil Berrigan; A. J. Muste; and John Howard Yoder. This proved a wellspring of the Catholic peace movement and opposition to the Vietnam War.

We poured more of the wine and apologized to Fr. Louis that it was not bourbon.

Uncle Louie's Porch

Merton's hermitage continues to be a setting for literary discussion among poets and writers. Merton continues to overshadow the dialogue, even if tacitly. I allow myself to take the liberty of calling him Uncle Louie because he himself once made that suggestion. When a lot of monks were changing their names—from such bizarre and obsolete names as Egbert, Amandus, or Bernadine to something more familiar—Fr. Louis said, "I don't care what you call me; you can call me Uncle Louie if you want." A few older and younger monks picked up on that. It serves well, and for a gathering of writers and meditators it is perfect.

Occasionally, prominent Kentucky authors visit the hermitage, such as Maurice Manning, poet (*The Common Man*) and winner of the Yale Younger Poets Prize; Silas House, the novelist (*Clay's Quilt*; *A Parchment of Leaves*); and Fenton Johnson, novelist and essayist (*The Man Who Loved Birds*; *Everywhere Home*). They usually come for an afternoon hike and an evening of readings. Sometimes a writer from out of state is present, such as Tracy Lee Simmons, Judith Valente (of NPR and a poet), or such prominent Canadian poets as Phil Hall, Marty Gervais, and John B. Lee. Several younger, newly published writers and theologians are likely to come as well, such as Dave Harrity, Justin Klassen, or Greg Hillis.

One particular gathering in December of 2015 was marked by a mishap. It was one of those stories that make for good literary history. The occasion was a visit of the novelist Fenton Johnson from the University of Arizona, where he teaches. He is originally from New Haven, Kentucky, three miles from the monastery, and he was visiting home. Fenton has an angular, almost anguished face combining features that remind me of Philip Glass and Albert Camus, hardly suggestive of the country boy he once was. He left our area at the age of seventeen, but his hometown and the abbey continue to be touchstones in his writing. We have had frequent discussions about poetry, solitude, and spirituality over the years. Many of our conversations have been about my favorite poets, Emily Dickinson and Rainer Maria Rilke, and Fenton's own favorite, Walt Whitman. Solitude, let alone celibacy, is hardly a popular topic these days, but his essay

"Going It Alone" had just appeared that autumn in *Harper's*, which in turn led to an interview on NPR's *Fresh Air*. He and I had spent an hour that morning talking about vows, another unlikely topic slated for a literary journal.

At the time of this December visit, Fenton was well along in recovery from cancer. The bane of long months of radiation was reported weekly to family and friends with an amazing wit and realism. But that was not to be the end of his woes. That gray afternoon started out robustly with five other Kentucky writers as we struck out through wintry woods covered with a heavy layer of dry leaves. I had forged on ahead with Greg Hillis, a scholar of Greek patristics from British Columbia, teaching at Bellarmine University. After five minutes no one seemed to be following us. Fenton was behind with Maurice Manning, Silas House, Jason Howard (editor of the literary quarterly *Appalachian Heritage*), and Dave Harrity (a poet with two books recently published). Soon I heard yelling, and Silas was chasing us down. Fenton had stepped into a groundhog hole buried under leaves, had fallen, and could not walk.

We found him with arms draped over the shoulders of the two biggest men, Maurice and Dave, hopping on one foot out of the woods toward his car. I was rendered speechless right up to the moment he departed. After all he had been through, and now this! Was it an act of God? Silas and Jason drove him to the emergency room, as it began to rain, leaving the rest of us sheltered on the porch, more thoughtful and subdued.

Fenton proved to have a horizontal crack in his leg bone at the ankle, and his foot was put in a boot cast painted red and white for the Christmas season. With time on his hands for recovery, he wrote a long piece he deemed to be "doggerel," a plaint against rodent foes of the human race. Since he solicited like commemoration, I took the occasion to write an apologia for "St. Theophilus," the underground recluse, rudely interrupted in his contemplative retreat.

Theophilus slept
in hermitage underground.
Giant's big mean foot
plunged rudely down his door,
made horrifying outcry,
disrupting repose—
mystical union
far beyond distinction of
groundhog and man.

A LIVING VISION

Before this tiny white hermitage was ever built, it was conceived as something larger than a place of solitude. Never
one to be one-dimensional, Fr. Louis had a vision of a place
where artists, intellectuals, activists, theologians, and monks
could come together for wholesome conversation. It would
afford a natural setting for an atmosphere of freedom and
relaxation, where there could be a meeting of minds without
any particular agenda. Today peacemakers, philosophers,
and the whole range of people described above continue to
be drawn here—drawn to openness, breadth of mind, and
breath of Spirit. Those who visit bring the best of what they
aspire to in life, hoping to find it reawakened in this unique
atmosphere. And often it is. This seems almost to happen of
its own accord, without anyone making a special point of it.

I doubt anyone included in this brief guest list would call
themselves holy or great, but to me they all seem so. Perhaps,
in its simplicity and authenticity, Fr. Louis's cinder-block
shelter—nothing much to look at in itself—functions as a
lens that focuses visitors on what they truly are. The place
speaks a truth of its own, something Fr. Louis often came
back to: our poverty and smallness. In such a place we find
our true self.

FINAL JUDGMENT

Given human nature as it is, my breezy days and years may finally spell out like those texts of scrambled words that you find on the web. These are sentences composed with each word containing all the correct letters but wrongly arranged. The surprising thing is that one can understand what it says if you don't read too closely. Just breeze through it and the mind picks up the meaning and gets the message.

Perhaps life is a chain of mistakes like that. When read carefully and closely, its days are confusing, wayward, and erroneous, but somehow God on a scan gets the sense of it. If my intention in life is love, I think that the meaning will get through.

Or maybe my life is like ancient Hebrew or Ugaritic script. The consonants are written, but the vowels are missing. Something has to be supplied and filled in. It is strange how modern texting devices have returned us full circle to stone tablets: just as stone proved too hard to chisel out the complete spelling, electronic devices are used by hands too busy to punch in all the letters—you have to read it in code.

Life, fully lived, expresses some kind of creativity. Some lives are written with beautiful penmanship, with well-honed skill expressing more than mere literal meaning, communicating the unique person as individually as a signature does. For other people, life is lived in a hurry-up state; it gets cut-and-pasted. Could there be creativity in tearing along and getting through it all anyhow? Will God smile at the fancy dance and see how cleverly we came through the scramble without losing the thread of meaning?

One seldom hears about "the last judgment" anymore: God's final judgment at the end of days. I seldom think about it myself. But when I do consider it, I prefer to think that it is not anything like a courtroom trial. That is something of this life; courtrooms belong to this world. In the next world, judgment will be more like an affirmation of truth, more like a grammatical statement that logicians call "a judgment." A judgment says something *is* something, or that something *is not* something. A judgment is a matter of getting down to what is definite.

If it comes to an ultimate pronouncement, what I am remains for God to say. In the end, it is not for me to say, for much that I imagine about myself is just that—a mirror in which I make faces. To say I am a sinner is a face to make. To say I'm not such a bad guy is another. Whatever is said is passing, uncertain, and mostly subjective. The point is, I make no judgment. Judgment is God's. As St. Paul said, "Therefore do not pronounce judgment before the time, before the Lord comes, who will bring to light the things now hidden in darkness, and will disclose the purposes of the heart" (1 Cor 4:5).

My part is to remain open and abandoned to what God brings for me to live out. For this, simplicity is essential, and the simplest thing of all is to accept to be. That is the most elemental thing about my life, and to practice being is what meditation is. It is more than a practice; it is life at its core—to rest fully in being. And to be fully is the rest of life. To live and breathe every day is intrinsically a gift, one that spells itself out in action. Or misspells at times. When every step in the dance is taken and completed, it is the whole that holds the meaning, no one part only.

God alone is pure act. My life is an exercise in being; it is a daily participation in and approximation to pure act. When it is authentic, it is a giving over to an astonishing freedom, the freedom to be a pure act of love. To love intentionally is to enter into the wholeness of God, who is "all in all" (1 Cor 15:28).

These reflections and stories about my life are another way of being present to my life intentionally. Not in order to relive it, but to re-create it as a form of celebration. To write is another form of prayer, in fact a rather laborious form, but like liturgy and labor, another way of entering into community with others, now in a haphazard way. It is useless in the same way as choir, and as prayer and meditation, is useless. It is a way of being in the present holding something, however small, of the whole that has been my life. Life has given me much to delight in, and I pass it on to others. "You received without payment; give without payment" (Mt 10:8).

St. Benedict said the first degree of humility is to live constantly in the eyes of God. Judgment is always looming over me. That begins as a fearful thing, and turns my mind away from what other people may think of me. To that extent it is the first step in freedom, and the standards of the world are of less importance, leave alone its opinions and prejudices. In the end this becomes a freedom and love that casts off fear. One remains in the eyes of God, but ultimately, who can read God's eyes? If you do not know love, you can never truly read the eyes of God.

Children want the attention of their parents while riding a bicycle for the first time—on that day when they can ride all on their own. It is as if what they are doing remains incomplete unless or until someone is watching: "Look, Mom, no hands!" "Oh, dear, be careful!" Mother responds. Who can read God's eyes? God's eyes are inscrutable unless read with love.

Epilogue

Fr. Louis once posed a question to a group of monks in training: "Did you get what you wanted when you came to the monastery?" It is a question worth posing to myself again some sixty years later.

The answers life gave me are surprising, and often out of line with what I thought I wanted. When I consider one of my peers in the novitiate, Fr. Timothy Kelly, I cannot conceive how he might have wanted the life he has now, fifty-eight years later—living in Rome and interacting with the Vatican as the Cistercian procurator. Likewise, I look at myself and think how surprising it is that I don't have things I sometimes thought I wanted: a primitive form of monasticism, a small community, some teaching work, more poverty and solitude. Then I look at truth and truth tells me, "You got what you have because you wanted it."

So what do I have? For the moment I have the moment. I am seated on a cedarwood chair on the porch of Merton's hermitage in the cool breeze of an August morning with the sound of a cuckoo bird back in the forest, where he presides with no concern for my affairs. I sit as if this is all I could ever know or care to know. There is nothing else to want. I listen to the cicadas and forget about wanting and not wanting. Such moments are themselves something worth wanting, but they do not come by wanting. They are a windfall.

This chair has a brass plate attached to the top: "Bench of Dreams." That plate was slapped on by a man of great dreams, Robert Muller, who had been assistant secretary-general of the United Nations for forty years. He founded the University for Peace in Costa Rica. The Thomas Merton Foundation brought him on a visit to Louisville and Gethsemani in preparation for the Thomas Merton Retreat in 2000. I cherish the brass plaque on this chair, quickly pulled out of the pocket and slapped on by that big-hearted man who lived immersed in the swirl of world events—someone who found kinship with a big-hearted monk who took refuge in this wooded solitude. So today this remains a porch touched by the United Nations, touched by the Dalai Lama, and by so many, many others.

However, at least for the time being, all seems perfectly unbusy here, except for the hummingbird at the feeder and branches nodding in the broken shade.

Ask me, "Have you found what you wanted in this life?" and I will likely pause and answer in the most essential sense, yes, I have. I basically wanted only one thing. The guiding principle that brought me here was, "Strive first for the kingdom of God and his righteousness, and all these things will be given you as well" (Mt 6:33). I wanted a simple life, quiet, and close to God. To put it more succinctly, I wanted *life*. To that, much has been added, well beyond my imaginings.

As for life lived in freedom and simplicity—I do get a bit of that every day. I make a point of slowing to a pause and staying there for a while. This short abiding yields greater ease in taking in the whole of life—the hundredfold that comes in addition. Without this essential quiet, monastic life (*any* life, I imagine) becomes a burden and a mess. Unless I stay focused on the one thing necessary, the rest can be unmanageable.

The question as to whether I got what I wanted is a false one. Most men come here with an obscure longing for—they don't know what. It is a nameless yearning, one that loses its authenticity when you start to explain it. What I felt then was only the beginning of something that God put in me. It was put there that God could teach me what to want. I have been learning ever since. When young visitors ask me what brought me to the monastery, I say I am still finding out. The monastery is a school of wanting, meant to take me beyond my mute desires into a deeper silence still—the inner repose of the heart where love itself instructs me in love. This school of charity has no graduation; there is nowhere to go afterwards, except to open the doors and allow others in.

There is nothing here to possess and claim because you wanted it. I am here only as somebody who was wanted, subtly and ineffably loved without my knowing how. This love dwells in and through my daily round of words and readings, rites, work, comings and goings, small courtesies, and petty complaints. In the midst of it, there is something bigger. People are crucial—with no exceptions—each person somehow contains the totality, but the totality is no one particular person. Nor is that the whole assembly of persons—monks old and new, departed and living, visitors, strangers, friends, workers, helpers. This complex hive with its steady, quiet buzz is not the totality, yet each one is more than just a particle of it. Each apparent particle is what it is, somehow, as a virtual immanence of the totality.

I have been brought into something larger than myself, larger than anything I could have wanted with my desires, likes, and dislikes, my ideals, dreams—with my choices, renunciations, world denials, asceticism, and restraints—all are insufficient to contain and corner it. This hundredfold, this windfall, demands a heart larger than my own, and my own heart is enhanced by it and grows larger, fitted for what is more. I might live to be one hundred and none of this will be finished.

For now, the best thing is to take in one breath at a time. And the next, and the next. Every breath comes from God, and the air supply is unlimited. Anxiety cramps my breath, my chest slumps over in mindless sloth. Social turmoil and fear create a smog of toxins; I have never seen a decade where there is no war. But you keep on breathing. And praying. Prayer is a breathing that purifies the air, like leaves on the tree. If I can do that for myself, I am most likely doing it for others. As a community breathing together, each leaf on the same tree, we raise the effect to an exponential level. The whole is greater than the sum of the parts.

Fortunately for me, this lush, verdant Kentucky countryside has plenty of wholesome air. And the monastery for over one hundred and fifty years has refreshed the atmosphere with persistent prayer. I have found this place to be a training resort for breathing in life again and again. We are surrounded with the good things that make life agreeable: good liturgy, good community, good order, plenty of reading and work—all of which are wholesome enough to be holy.

The choreography of the day, the week, and the year sets my pace and keeps me going. What monastics call "the regular life" is also a form of play. I dance in the water of time, with its threat of sinking, but I am breathing the air of the timeless. The arm strokes, the leg kicks, and the repetition keep me afloat and breathing easier, buoyant on the margin of time and eternity.

CODA

Save, O God, this vagrant seeking You
from ever finding You. Find me rather
in Your ceaseless search
where I already am.

Draw me with You into
Your vagabond life,
forever searching and forever finding,
and make it mine.

Relieve me of wanting and having,
my ever having and wanting. Take me into
the circle dance of Your freedom
which never searches
and never possesses.

In You to seek and to find are ever one.
In You seeking and finding never are.
How can I seek what is already here?
How can I find what never was lost?

NOTES

INTRODUCTION TO THE CIRCLE DANCE

page 1   "Man's unhappiness . . ." Blaise Pascal, *Pensées and Other Writings*, trans. Honor Levi, ed. Anthony Levi (New York: Oxford University Press, 1995), 44.

page 2   All quotations from the Rule of St. Benedict are taken from *St. Benedict's Rule for Monasteries*, trans. Leonard J. Doyle (Collegeville, MN: Liturgical Press, 1948).

page 4   "We have but to live . . ." Matthew Kelty, *Sermons in a Monastery: Chapter Talks*, ed. William O. Paulsell (Kalamazoo, MI: Cistercian Publications, 1983), 106.

page 6   "[L]et go of our own obsession with what . . ." Merton, *New Seeds of Contemplation*, 296–97.

page 7   "He outstripped Time with but a Bout . . ." *The Poems of Emily Dickinson: Reading Edition*, ed. Ralph W. Franklin (Cambridge, Mass.: The Belknap Press of Harvard University Press, 1998), #1111.

A Life of Song and Music

page 19   "Your music alone . . ." is one of my unpublished poems.

page 19   "Here my breathless Alleluias, in triple ascent . . ." also appears in my collection *Laughter: My Purgatory* (Windsor, ON: Black Moss Press, 2002), 13.

Thomas Merton, Novice Master

page 28   "I must say there is a good proportion . . ." *Thomas Merton: A Life in Letters*, ed. William H. Shannon and Christine M. Bochen (Notre Dame, IN: Ave Maria Press, 2010), 179–80.

Nature, My Guru

page 42   "O Sweet Irrational Worship," Thomas Merton, *Emblems of a Season of Fury* (Norfolk, CT: J. Laughlin, 1963).

page 42   ["There is a place you can go . . ."] "are themselves / your thoughts," Wendell Berry, *This Day: Collected and New Sabbath Poems* (Berkeley, CA: Counterpoint Press, 2014), 190.

A Week at the Hermitage

page 46   My poem "Restless Silence" appears in *Unquiet Vigil: New and Selected Poems* (Brewster, MA: Paraclete Press, 2014), 78–79.

Prayer Nutures Poetry

page 82   "I don't know exactly what a prayer is . . ." Mary Oliver, *New and Selected Poems, Volume One* (Boston: Beacon Press, 2004), 94.

page 82   "Tell all the truth . . ." *The Poems of Emily Dickinson: Reading Edition*, #1263.

page 82   "One dark night . . ." *John of the Cross: Selected Writings*, ed. Kieran Kavanaugh (Mahwah, NJ: Paulist Press, 1988), 61.

Battle of Wits with a Mockingbird

page 88   "The crowded stars . . ." G. K. Chesterton, *Orthodoxy*, (New York: John Lane Company, 1908), 107.

Emily Dickinson, Soul Sister

page 91   "Growth of Man . . ." *The Poems of Emily Dickinson: Reading Edition*, #790; "I live with Him," #698.

page 92   "Experience is the Angled Road," *The Poems of Emily Dickinson: Reading Edition*, #788.

page 93   "Publication — is the Auction," *The Poems of Emily Dickinson: Reading Edition*, #788

page 94   "To earn it by disdaining it," *The Poems of Emily Dickinson: Reading Edition*, #1445

page 95   "A solemn thing — it was," *The Poems of Emily Dickinson: Reading Edition*, #307; "The

Maker of the soul," #877; "The Soul's Superior instants," #630;

page 97   "He fumbles at your Soul," *The Poems of Emily Dickinson: Reading Edition*, #477; "This Consciousness that is aware," #817; "I cling to nowhere till I fall," #1532;

page 98   "As if the Sea should part," *The Poems of Emily Dickinson: Reading Edition*, #720; "Their Height in Heaven comforts not," #725; "Narcotics cannot still the Tooth," #373.

page 98   "My own flesh and blood, my own kind of quiet rebel . . ." Thomas Merton, *A Search for Solitude: The Journals of Thomas Merton, Volume Three, 1952–1960*, ed. Lawrence S. Cunningham (San Francisco: HarperSanFrancisco, 1997), 364.

CONTEMPLATION AND THE CAMERA

page 108   My poem "The Cowl," also appears in *Unquiet Vigil*, 105.

MERTON'S DEATH AS SEEN FROM THE HOME GROUNDS

page 109   A modified version of this essay also appears in *What I Am Living For: Lessons from the Life and Writings of Thomas Merton* (Notre Dame, IN: Ave Maria Press 2018).

page 111   "I never thought to have had . . ." Merton, *A Search for Solitude*, 372.

page 111   "I am not going 'home'. . ." Thomas Merton, *The Other Side of the Mountain: The Journals of Thomas Merton, Volume Seven, 1967–1968*, ed. Patrick Hart, O.C.S.O. (San Francisco: HarperSanFrancisco, 1997), 174.

page 116   "That you may become the brother of God . . ." Thomas Merton, *The Seven Storey Mountain* (New York: Mariner Books, 1999), 462.

page 117   "I came to Gethsemani December 10 . . ." Thomas Merton, *The School of Charity: The Letters of Thomas Merton on Religious Renewal and Spiritual Direction*, ed. Br. Patrick Hart (New York: Mariner Books, 1993), 7.

UNEXPECTED VISITORS

page 120   "I cannot live with You . . ." *The Poems of Emily Dickinson: Reading Edition*, #760.

page 122   "Nuns of Avila misunderstood . . ." Quenon, *Unquiet Vigil*, 97.

CODA

page 137   "Coda" is one of my unpublished poems.

Other works by Paul Quenon:

Unquiet Vigil

The Art of Pausing

Bells of the Hours

Monkswear

Afternoons with Emily

Laughter My Purgatory

Holy Folly

Terrors of Paradise

Br. Paul Quenon, O.C.S.O., entered the Trappists in 1958 at the Abbey of Gethsemani in Kentucky, where Thomas Merton was his novice master. Quenon is a photographer and the author of several books of poetry, including *Unquiet Vigil*—named a "Best Spiritual Book of the Year" by *Spirituality & Practice* and "Best Poetry Volume of the Year" by Hearts and Minds Books. Quenon coauthored *Carved in Stone* and also contributed spiritual reflections to other books.

Pico Iyer is a British author and *Time* magazine essayist who lives in Japan.